Also by Marge Piercy

Poetry

AVAILABLE LIGHT
MY MOTHER'S BODY
STONE, PAPER, KNIFE
CIRCLES ON THE WATER
THE MOON IS ALWAYS FEMALE
THE TWELVE-SPOKED WHEEL FLASHING
LIVING IN THE OPEN
TO BE OF USE
4-TELLING (with Robert Hershon, Emmett Jarrett, Dick Lourie)
HARD LOVING
BREAKING CAMP

Novels

HE, SHE AND IT
SUMMER PEOPLE
GONE TO SOLDIERS
FLY AWAY HOME
BRAIDED LIVES
VIDA
THE HIGH COST OF LIVING
WOMAN ON THE EDGE OF TIME
SMALL CHANGES
DANCE THE EAGLE TO SLEEP
GOING DOWN FAST

Other

THE LAST WHITE CLASS: A PLAY (with Ira Wood)
PARTI-COLORED BLOCKS FOR A QUILT: ESSAYS
EARLY RIPENING: AMERICAN WOMEN'S POETRY NOW;
  AN ANTHOLOGY
THE EARTH SHINES SECRETLY: A BOOK OF DAYS
  (with paintings by Nell Blaine)

ND HER CHILDREN

Poems by Marge Piercy

ALFRED A. KNOPF   New York   1994

THIS IS A BORZOI BOOK
PUBLISHED BY ALFRED A. KNOPF, INC.

Copyright © 1992 by Middlemarsh, Inc.

All rights reserved under International and Pan-American Copyright Conventions. Published in the United States by Alfred A. Knopf, Inc., New York, and simultaneously in Canada by Random House of Canada Limited, Toronto. Distributed by Random House, Inc., New York.

Various poems in this collection originally appeared in the following publications: *American Poetry Review, Boston Review, Calapooya Collage, Cape Cod Driftlines, Caprice, Chiron Review, Colorado Review, Columbia, The Creative Woman, Croton Review, The Earth Shines Secretly: A Book of Days, Footwork, Frontiers, Gopherwood Review, Images, Key West Review, Lunar Calendar, Matrix, Michigan Quarterly Review, Mississippi Mud, Ms., Nightsun, Organic Gardening, Poetry East, Poets On, The Poets Perspective, Slant, The Sow's Ear, Sycamore Review, Taos Review, Tikkun, Visions International, Woman of Power, Yellow Silk, Zone 3.*

Library of Congress Cataloging-in-Publication Data
Piercy, Marge.
Mars and her children : poems / by Marge Piercy. — 1st ed.
p. cm.
ISBN 0-679-41004-X
ISBN 0-679-73877-0 (pbk.)
I. Title.
PS3566.I4M37   1992
811'.54—dc20   91-29247
                                                                      CIP

Manufactured in the United States of America

Published April 23, 1992
Reprinted Once
Third Printing, July 1994

Mars and Her Children

MARS

Contents

Mars and Her Children

The ark of consequence

The classic rainbow shows as an arc,
a bridge strung in thinning clouds,
but I have seen it flash a perfect circle,
rising and falling and rising again
through the octave of colors,
a sun shape rolling like a wheel of light.

Commonly it is a fraction of a circle,
a promise only partial, not a banal
sign of safety like a smile pin,
that rainbow cartoon affixed to vans
and baby carriages. No, it promises
only, this world will not self-destruct.

Account the rainbow a boomerang of liquid
light, foretelling rather that what we
toss out returns in the water table;
flows from the faucet into our bones.
What we shoot up into orbit falls
to earth one night through the roof.

Think of it as a promise that what
we do continues in an arc
of consequence, flickers in our
children's genes, collects in each

spine and liver, gleams in the apple,
coats the down of the drowning auk.

When you see the rainbow iridescence
shiver in the oil slick, smeared
on the waves of the poisoned river,
shudder for the covenant broken, for we
are given only this floating round ark
with the dead moon for company and warning.

VIOLET

Fox grapes

It is near the railroad bridge over the creek
where wild blue grapes run rampant up trees,
the ones the locals call fox grapes.
I have seen you pick them with your teeth.

You are poised in the old right of way,
your body a straight line out to the plume's tip
but for your jack of diamond's face, pointed,
wary, jutting at me sharp as a glass corner.

Our eyes meet. We stand each with our feet
loaded and ready to discharge into motion.
That look is opaque and piercing and curious.
We drink each other like whiskey, straight

and strong and blinding in the brain.
For a long time we hold each other stabbed
through as if by desire. Then you stir
and are gone in the baked grasses. All day

nothing human of words or touch pierces my brain
to that deep spot where your ember smoulders.
Your family is breaking. You start your wild
solitary fall when you hunt and run alone.

Softly during the night

Rain is tickling the leaves like the ghost of itself.
I wake to it and at first I think it is someone
muttering in my ear. It is a teasing caress
on the roof, a lover's hair brushing my belly,
a cat who raps your arm lightly with her tail
to call back your attention from the trivial book.

When I went to bed, the moon was bobbing, sinking
on long breaking waves of cloud. Salt hung
in the air, lightly stinging the eyes and nostrils.
Now it is dark in the fringed shawl of the rain.
I lie awake listening, for its liquid whisper
snags the attention more closely than clamor,

rain that slips in on the sly. The dawn sky
will be mauve, cloudless, clean as a new tent
just raised. Only the leaves on the roadside
bushes brushing my face with heavy drops of water
as I pass bear witness to what came and left
furtive as if it took instead of giving.

Bell song

Ah, the body. It is a great
bronze bell. It looks solid.
Inert, asleep, it hangs there,
something no breeze even tips,
something no casual touch can wake.

But when it moves, when it is rung
the sound waves pass through walls.
It vibrates down into the bedrock,
the air itself rolls in surges
that make the bones resound.

For a while everything is realigned,
new magnetic poles in the spine
and the fingertips. Then the body
tolls, this is what I am for.
Peal me again, again, again.

Thinking of Homer at twilight

Dark Harbor: Penny wore that phrase
on a tee shirt bought in Maine
on an island. I think of black pearl water,
of entering a steep fiord under a mountain.
Perhaps it was where boats put in late;
or perhaps it was the first to lose the sun.

Perhaps the rocks color the water,
as I remember a narrow rocky cove
wedge shaped on Kerkyra where the granite
angled under and the water looked
red wine dark, me quoting Homer of course.
I was a frequent quoter in those days.

Homer worked in an oral tradition,
as did my story-telling grandmother whose eyes
were white as boiled egg with cataracts,
but I write. Conventionalized dense squiggles
are how I translate the world, how I
transform energy into matter into energy.

Dark Harbor: for me the phrase evokes fright,
that penultimate fear of the dark that has
shadowed my poor vision since childhood.
"You're going to read yourself blind,"
my mother warned, upset when the school
insisted she buy me spectacles.

How would I move about? How could I live
without the sight of maple leaves, roses,

the face of my lover, sunlight burning
the wave tips, the agouti pelt of the bay
in winter breathing in slow heaves.
The sun blinds me I say but it only dazzles.

I can get drunk on color, lured like a bee
to drench myself in reds and blues and purples,
to taste the shades of green in the spring woods
like a mesclune lightly dressed with vinegar,
to roll over the eyeball the hues stirred
in the wave as the tongue sorts a good wine.

With my poor patched vision I have taught
myself to observe, to clutch, to snatch
at color and shape and line and lineament.
When can I see you? Do you see what I mean?
Far-seeing visionary. A psychic blind spot.
I too conflate seeing, knowing, understanding.

I think of my father who could not tell
night from day, lost in a dimness swirling
in eyes and brain, tripping if a chair was moved
a foot from its spot on his inner map.
I no longer drive at night: scenarios
of the impossible sap me to despair.

Grey has always been my color of mourning,
of despair, of ash, of indecision,
of desperate stratagems, of muted survival,
the color of dirty fog at twilight dissolving

the world into second guesses, missed turnings.
Glaucoma is quiet, subtle, like radiation.

The blindness swells, an acid fog loosed
from genes, trouble from both sides, inexorable
as age. I try to steer my leaking craft
in the storm bearing down, praying, begging
to stay tossed in the open light lashed sea,
out of the dark harbor, still water waiting.

The seduction of anticipated pain

You rush to embrace a certain
form of pain like a bright tempered sword
focusing light into a point of blindness
on which you impale yourself.

You thrust into that pain
as into an iron maiden, yank it closed
so that its spikes tear through flesh,
organs until they meet like the grin

of a shark. This is reality,
you say as you bleed there in the dark
of the grinding teeth, this is how
I always secretly knew it would come out.

This is what I am shaped for, the act
for which I have been grown as the apple
is planted to be eaten; I was bred
and hand-raised to this like the pheasant

the state scatters corn to in its pens,
then drops at the roadside in October
to be slaughtered by hunters with shotguns
to whom he runs, hungry, asking for corn.

Outside in the woods of the world, my love,
an owl carries a vole as a pledge to its mate,

the petals of the wild apple tree speckle
the sand and the kingfisher strikes like passion

in feathers to rise with a moon glint of fish.
The only world is neither unjust nor just
but round as an apple and we are made of it
to wonder, to savor and struggle and hurt,

to think, to try to build justice as the beaver
builds her dam, to weather the seasons,
the random bolts of nuisance and disaster, to love
what we can and endure in light and darkness.

Waking with my ears ringing

Sometimes I wake up in the night.
I squint at the green-eyed clock
and it tells me two fourteen. Outside
rain sidles down. Why does my head
ring with shouting? Words, loud words
have been thrown tumbling like empty
boxes down the steps of my spine.

Who argues in my head at night
after I have crawled into the wet
cave of my own belly to sleep?
My cats snooze in a multicolored heap,
one snoring, one whimpering. My
love is chewing the cud of his day
grinding his teeth and mumbling.

But my brain bears the scuff marks of boots.
Somebody has been pacing there ranting—
the dogmatist I was at thirty-two?
Noisy ghosts have been making speeches.
Are these sins of omission screeching?
Unworn alternate selves in chartreuse?
Scorned opinions demanding equal air time?

I am like the beds in rooming houses
of World War II Detroit in the housing crisis
of my childhood, slept on in turns,
one guy getting into bed from the graveyard
shift when another crawled out to shower.
My head is in continuous use, rented out
to ghosts whenever I shut off the lights.

What crosses over

The deep dark waters of the belly
shudder into pleasure, swirling
in a whirlpool which discharges strange
swallowed creatures miles and days hence.

Sometimes in the afternoon dusky tent
of the bed, in the slithering night
when stars press into our eyes
like droplets of fine hot ice

falling through the softened bones
of the skull into the shining brain,
thoughts flow across the membranes
like any other fluid exchanged.

I know you then, as I know the taste
of peaches, the alphabet of your spine.

Report of the Fourteenth Subcommittee on Convening a Discussion Group

This is how things begin to tilt into change,
how coalitions are knit from strands of hair,
of barbed wire, twine, knitting wool and gut,
how people ease into action arguing each inch,
but the tedium of it is watching granite erode.

Let us meet to debate meeting, the day, the time,
the length. Let us discuss whether we will sit
or stand or hang from the ceiling or take it lying
down. Let us argue about the chair and the table and
the chairperson and the motion to table the chair.

In the room fog gathers under the ceiling and thickens
in every brain. Let us form committees spawning
subcommittees all laying little moldy eggs of reports.
Under the grey fluorescent sun they will crack
to hatch scuttling lizards of more committees.

The Pliocene gathers momentum and fades.
The earth tilts on its axis. More and more snows
fall each winter and less melt each spring.
A new ice age is pressing the glaciers forward
over the floor. We watch the wall of ice advance.

We are evolving into molluscs, barnacles
clinging to wood and plastic, metal and smoke

while the stale and flotsam-laden tide of rhetoric
inches up the shingles and dawdles back.
This is true virtue: to sit here and stay awake,

to listen, to argue, to wade on through the muck
wrestling to some momentary small agreement
like a pinhead pearl prized from a dragon-oyster.
I believe in this democracy as I believe
there is blood in my veins, but oh, oh, in me

lurks a tyrant with a double-bladed ax who longs
to swing it wide and shining, who longs to stand
and shriek, You Shall Do as I Say, pig-bastards.
No more committees but only picnics and orgies
and dances. I have spoken. So be it forevermore.

Do not erect the wall
before yourselves

for Carolyn Forché and Harry Mattison

You walked through the supermarket shelves,
back through the bright packages labeled with grinning
pink and purple cartoon bears and boxes shining
like desire itself, much too large for what's within;
you walked through the display of bananas in bright
sunny pyramids, into the flesh of the mango
and it bled into your eyes and made them burn.

In the back room of the supermarket, you say,
your hands seeking themselves, wrestling
in your lap, your eyes opaque with shining
like the eyes of the great endangered cats in the dark,
the bodies hung up for butchering and neat packaging
are human. These wondrous identical melons
are fertilized from the slit throats of Indians.

From El Salvador, from South Africa you return,
fire still singeing the paper you pick up idly.
Here it is quiet but the ringing in your ears
is really someone screaming behind a metal door.
You tell me you have seen the future of power,
that enough killing kills the dream in the bone's
marrow, for flesh cannot stand against lasers.

If you butcher a man's mother, he fights you.
If you kill a woman's baby before her, she fights
you and with each slaughter you anneal the survivors
into rebellion. But they have learned, you say,
to be more efficient for if you kill everyone

in a valley, if you blow up their houses and machine
gun even their animals; or you simply shut them

into a camp and starve them to death,
it goes on quietly until they are all gone.
This is not an allegory, you say, it is right
now. We are both thinking of Auschwitz
and Sobibor, and you say you grasp
now how people did not really care to notice.
The pain of others is the noise of traffic passing.

Despair coils into itself, twilight opalescent
conch shell leading to a still dark chamber
at the center secret and vulnerable as a pharaoh's
tomb. The young poets at your reading adored
the savage pain and broken bodies in the imagery
but stubbornly ignored what you meant; they like
violence in rhetoric, confused with sex.

I beg you not to erect Moloch, for evil too
is merely partial, confused. They are never
thorough enough to kill the whole body of earth.
History flows like salt from the ancestral ocean
in the blood and hope is carried like oxygen
in iron. We are an ancient organism groping
toward light. We are the children of want,

of lives once smashed down into the peasant mud,
of short generations stunted by hunger like scrub

oaks never free from the storm wind, of women
whose breasts dribbled thin pain into baby's mouths,
women broken like the stems of tulips blooming
too early. We carry all those lives in us,
eggs in an alewife that must keep thrashing upstream.

Of the patience called forth by transition

Notice how the sky is a milky opal
cloudless from rim to rim, of an indefinite
height and sliding now at midafternoon
into darkness. Pearly, it melts
imperceptibly into yellow and green,
willow colors from another season,
or the yellow of aspen leaves already fallen,
into lavender now, the sea lavender
shriveled in the marshes. As the trees
reduce themselves to bony gesture
and the woods echo the hues of earth
itself, the colors of the light must feed
our eye's hunger, the ruddy sun of winter.

In early spring, we look down for color,
we look for the green of skunk cabbage,
golden crocuses along the south walls,
the small ears of violets unfolding.
Before the snows that glaze and magnify,
glitter and transmute, we look upwards.
Great Chinese peonies float over the bay
splendid, bronzed by the light rebounding
from the water. In November we gaze up
into the stormy garden of the clouds.
What comes to us rides on the wind
and we face into it like gulls, waiting.

Dreaming the frog's sleep

I think of all the cold ones,
the worms wriggling beneath the sodden earth
that freezes downward under the plaster
ceiling of snow, thick, white, bas-relief
intricate ice sketches of the dead.

I wonder at the frogs creeping
together to wait out the freeze under
the bridge; the turtles whose hearts beat
as slow as the moon wanes, buried in mud.
In the chrysalis aping a bud on a branch,
the bright blossom of butterfly cooks inside.

The cold-blooded ones, they use the sun
to jump-start their bodies. We think
our hot blood means we are superior.
Our predators kill many times over,
heaps of corpses to stoke the heart's furnace.

We assume being active is better
than being passive, a portion ascribed
by men to women, colonizers to natives.
Blood and bone, they join their flesh
with winter while we skate
on the surface shivering.

At the new moon: Rosh Hodesh

Once a two day holiday, the most sacred stretches
in the slow swing of the epicycling year;
then a remnant, a half holiday for women,
a little something to keep us less unsatisfied;
then abandoned at enlightenment along with herbals
and amulets, bobbe-mysehs, grandmothers' stories.

Now we fetch it up from the bottom of the harbor,
a bone on which the water has etched itself,
and from this bone we fashion a bird, extinct
and never yet born, evolving feathers
from our hair, blood from our salt, strength
from our backs, vision from our brains.

Fly out over the city, dove of the light,
owl of the moon, for we are weaving your wings
from our longings, diaphanous and bony.
Pilots and rabbis soared. The only females
to fly were witches and demons, the power
to endure and the power to destroy alone

granted us. But we too can invent,
can make, can do, undo. Here we stand
in a circle, the oldest meeting, the shape
women assume when we come together
that echoes ours, the flower, the mouth,
breast, opening, pool, the source.

We greet the moon that is not gone
but only hidden, unreflecting, inturned
and introspective, gathering strength to grow

as we greet the first slim nail paring
of her returning light. Don't we understand
the strength that wells out of retreat?

Can we not learn to turn in to our circle,
to sink into the caves of our silence,
to drink lingering by those deep cold wells,
to dive into the darkness of the heart's storm
until under the crashing surge of waves
it is still except for our slow roaring breath?

We need a large pattern of how things change
that shows us not a straight eight-lane tearing
through hills blasted into bedrock; not stairs
mounting to the sacrificial pyramid where hearts
are torn out to feed the gods of power, but the coil
of the moon, that epicycling wheel

that grows fat and skinny, advances and withers,
four steps forward and three back, and yet nothing
remains the same, for the mountains are piled up
and worn down, for the rivers eat into the stone
and the fields blow away and the sea makes sand
spits and islands and carries off the dune.

Let the half day festival of the new moon
remind us how to retreat and grow strong, how to
reflect and learn, how to push our bellies forward,
how to roll and turn and pull the tides up, up
when we need them, how to come back each time
we look dead, making a new season shine.

RED

Apple sauce for Eve

Those old daddies cursed you and us in you,
damned for your curiosity: for your sin
was wanting knowledge. To try, to taste,
to take into the body, into the brain
and turn each thing, each sign, each factoid
round and round as new facets glint and white
fractures into colors and the image breaks
into crystal fragments that pierce the nerves
while the brain casts the chips into patterns.

Each experiment sticks a finger deep in the pie,
dares existence, blows a horn in the ear
of belief, lets the nasty and difficult brats
of real questions into the still air
of the desiccated parlor of stasis.
What we all know to be true, constant,
melts like frost landscapes on a window
in a jet of steam. How many last words
in how many dead languages would translate into,
But what happens if I, and Whoops!

We see Adam wagging his tail, good dog, good
dog, while you and the snake shimmy up the tree,
lab partners in a dance of will and hunger,
that thirst not of the flesh but of the brain.
Men always think women are wanting sex,

cock, snake, when it is the world she's after.
The birth trauma for the first conceived kid
of the ego, I think therefore I am, I
kick the tree, who am I, why am I,
going, going to die, die, die.

You are indeed the mother of invention,
the first scientist. Your name means
life: finite, dynamic, swimming against
the current of time, tasting, testing,
eating knowledge like any other nutrient.
We are all the children of your bright hunger.
We are all products of that first experiment,
for if death was the worm in that apple,
the seeds were freedom and the flowering of choice.

Runt vigor

This apple tree was born of accident
a core tossed, seeds dropped in the bushes
under a pine that should have smothered it.

But it grew sideways, bowing out
like a great letter J, horizontally
snaking along the ground seeking release

before it rose free, snatching sunlight.
Deformed, a vigorous woodland monster,
its fragrance softens the spring mist.

It raises a lace tent among the pines,
salmon buds, flowers white as a wedding.
All November the deer taste its fruit.

Core memory

Apple core: dark eye seeds
carry the life of the past
into the future,
release a faint taste of almond—
cyanide?—when I bite into them.

In the magic cuneiform of the genes is written
the color of our eyes, length of lashes,
glaucoma, troubles we will not know till sixty,
the curve of the hipbones' kettle, the knobs
of the knees, our secret knowledge how to heal,
instructions to the liver and pituitary,
intricate code of the enzymes.

A scroll the years unfurl
as we try to rewrite it: little shocks
cross the gap one dawn from the bathroom mirror.
Daddy's jowls. Aunt Selma's eyelids.

The mind's a palimpsest in which early rough
sketches colored crudely as Sunday comics—
cartoons of women giving birth through navels,
flying skulls, superheroes dressed in blue condoms—
throb under the fretwork of education.
Old punishments still smoulder like a tire dump.

Core memory: what controls urges, whims, fears
from its hideaway bunker over the spine.
There early we learned, I cry and it happens then;

I close my eyes and it goes away; I scream
and the breast comes sweet with milk.
There gleam the eyes that watch,
God, mommy, big daddy.

How can I reprogram that greedy brat—
manipulative screamer pulling
on the nerves till they bong like Big Ben
and the head reverberates with obsolete need?
My worst enemy is encoded in my body
yearning for fats, sugar, salt,
with lava thick anger and fear
of the strange like a stupid watchdog
yapping all night at passing cars
indifferent to who is inside them.

Dream of white and red poppies

Drifts of white poppy blow on the foaming wind.
The petals quilt the loam. The stripped center
bulges darkly and leaks a delicate resin.
I taste mohn, poppyseed filling. Freckled breads.

Red poppies are brief and vehement in the yard.
A strong wind dismembers them in minutes.
A hard rain tosses scarlet satin scarves
dipped in black down into the mud. I regret

I did not take them when I could, sever
their stems, sear them in the gas flame
and put them in vases, snatching every one.
My restraint means I'll wait twelve months.

I regret my abstinence: butterflies'
silk wings scattered by storm on the dune.

Blood lake

Near Marquette, the plane circling
like a harrier stoops suddenly
through the false lake of clouds.
All dimensions vanish in grey.
Then below I see Mars.

In Chicago it was tulip spring.
People took off their jackets.
Here the snow stretches unbroken.
The firs are black,
the rock rimmed lake bright red.

Other lakes are frozen,
crosshatched
with tire tracks,
stubbled with shanties.
Not this one. Whatever
dyed its bloodshot eyeball
doesn't freeze. The river
snaking into it steams,
red ochre like rock
paintings left on cliffs
when the land was whole.

Ominous, bright with poison
this torn landscape fascinates:

the skeleton of a deer
I stumbled on in the lee
of a dune at home, the arrow
that sucked its life out
lying across the scoured ribs
arched, an ancient shipwreck,
the skull spare and elegant
as a Japanese garden.

Cousin, Cousine

How many chimpanzees does it take
to screw off the head of a researcher
who thinks callousness is the scientific
method?

In cages in laboratories, in primate research centers
chimpanzees and apes are signing, signing,
hello, hello, my name is Washo, my name is Michael,
hello, when will my teacher come back?
Where is computer? Talk to me please please.

Help, lonely cold. Mary good girl, good.
Play-speak. Please, please. But research money
for communicating has dried up. We resent
those bright hairy cartoons signaling us.

Employees in primate labs keep quitting:
janitors, the people who feed and clean cages
find the work disturbing, demeaning; they have
bad dreams. Those eyes watch them back.

In Oklahoma I heard of a woman who carried many
chimpanzees back to Africa and was living herself
in a cage on an island. The chimpanzees lived free

outside, once she taught them to forage.
The mothers all stayed with her in a tight band.

They would not leave her. But the children left.
The children swinging off in new bands.
Now we are talking about tearing the hearts
out of chimpanzees to replace bad human hearts.

Vlad the Impaler had a relative who drank
the blood of young women because she thought
it kept her beautiful. So do we drink the world's
bright blood out of terminal vanity.

The young women were peasants: she had a right
to their blood, she believed. Tell me how
it is different, how those beings signaling, talking,
waving to us, are ours to use as walking organ
banks, how we can give them AIDS and endless pain.

Like little firecrackers
in the brain

June morning hot as fresh coffee just poured.
The sun bakes the field of wild rose, virginiana,
till the air shimmers with that scent, sensual,
sexual, as if we were bees drawn drunken
into the heart of the petals to the pistil.

Provence floats just over the sand of the Cape:
Provence where they harvest flowers like corn
to distill into perfume, precious essence
of summer's blood, till neat stucco streets,
red tiled roofs and plane trees reek of roses.

We are fast-walking in damp swampy woods
where white azaleas exude creamy nectar
until we push harder as if the air thickened.
Then on the old railroad right-of-way, Halls'
honeysuckle clambers over the poison ivy.

Morning sun burns each flower into haze
that laves the brain in its essence
pressing inward till memory flares, spreads:
nostalgia, desire, regret, lilies in bright
primary colors and pastels, opening wide.

Your father's fourth heart attack

The phone cord is the umbilicus
that binds him dying, shriveled,
to you his first son.
You try to draw him to you.
You give him advice. I hear

your voice tender, careful,
admonishing, arguing.
You ask him ten polite ways
why he is killing himself
by the teaspoonful, by the drop,

by the puff. Why he eats
ashes instead of apples,
why he sucks on death's
icy dry tit, why he turns
his face into darkness.

You cajole him, a step, a step
like a father coaxing a toddler,
but he falls through your fingers
into a maze of knives giving him
his face back screaming.

Twelve hours a day he worked,
four hours commuting, up nights
in a chair by TV late show light
wolfing burnt steak and salami on rye,
counting other men's paychecks.

He lived among men with boats,
sleek men, slick men, always richer.
He bought a boat from a moneyed neighbor,

40

fiberglass hulled, had it repaired,
started it, roared out and sank.

No place he lived was ever right,
but he was always talking up the next
move. He quarreled with brothers,
mother, friends, son, in-laws,
everyone except the bosses he twisted

and wrang himself to please.
He was always hungry. If he ate five
sandwiches, his hunger still knocked
on his bones like a broken radiator
and he was never full.

He lived a hunger bigger than a man,
a hunger to be other, golden,
a hollowness finally now filled
with pain. He holds you in the phone
but his eyes seek the dark in the mirror.

He slips in and out of his deathbed
like a suit he keeps trying on, refitting.
He grabs at a hand and speaks the wrong
name, and the hand flops cold as a fish
while he calls till hoarseness, for himself.

Cast skins

The snake casts its skin on the sand track.
Its new skin is a bright, fresh-painted
fresco; its old skin rapidly fades, colors
vanishing. It dries and blows away,
shredded to dust on the brown grass of drought.
Plumage a hawk plucked from a sparrow.
Tufts a sheep rubbed on a standing stone.

Worn red leather gloves still plump with absent
fists, sketch as they lie on a table
the gestures of dead hands that chafed them.
Seductive, beckoning, the fingers arch
over furry caves. Lifted to the nose
a faint steam of perfume rises and is gone.
Maybe only memory leaked that scent.

On the back of the door a faded bathrobe
draws in upon itself, as if in modesty
held shut. New it was loud as a neighbor's
dance party, but washing subdued it pale,
respectable, red and purple roses lolling
with desire given a salt cure. It says
still, see me, see my body, it's crying.

Women's hopes congeal in old lipstick tubes,
creams the Avon lady brought her, perfumes
with the names of garden flowers, gardenia,
carnation, lily of the valley, rose.
They share drawers with clippings about women

who won a million dollars in cereal box
contests, home cures for bursitis.

When I was poor and shopped Salvation Army
stores for clothes and housewares, I used
to think I could hear the clothes whispering
in piles the dreams of women who discarded them,
this is the dress in which he did not love me,
this is the coat that never kept me warm
from the wind of need and anxiety's icy tweak.

The scorned bodies of hundreds of women
crowded there hanging on the subway cars
of racks, laid thrashing on the tables, pawed,
tossed up, thrown down. The air was sour
with disappointment, betrayal, weight lost
and gained hanging in fatty clouds.
Women buy clothes as a form of prayer

to a god never satisfied by offered flesh.
Her clothes even as I bundle them up
say she did not love them, never loved
them, and they always knew they would end up
on the marked down rummage tables at Good Will
where other women will buy them as body
bandages to sit out life in, to wait to die.

Up and out

1. The foot gnawed off

We occupy neighborhoods like rooming houses.
The Irish lived here; the Italians, then the Jews,
then the Blacks up from the South and now
the Vietnamese fill this dirty decaying motel.
Nobody imagines staying. Success means getting out.

To be in a place then is only a move in a game;
who can love a box on a board? Remaining
is being stuck. My parents amused themselves
all through my childhood by choosing houses
from the Sunday paper to visit.

They could not afford to buy but pretended.
They wanted to walk through the large rooms
of their fantasies criticizing the wallpaper,
counting other people's chairs, imagining
waking in that bedroom on that street.

How can we belong to ourselves, when home
is something to pry yourself out of
like a pickup stuck on a sand road;
when what holds you has to be sacrificed
as a fox will gnaw off a foot to be free.

Growing up, what you love most can trap you.
Friends are for discarding. Lovers

for saying good-bye. Marriage looks like a closet.
Even your faithful dog could slow you down.
Polish your loneliness until its headlight shines.

Always what formed you, those faces
that hung like ripe apples in the tree
of your childhood: the hands that caressed you,
whose furtive touch untied the knot of pleasure
and loosened your flesh till it fluttered

and streamed with joy; those who taught you
fear at the end of a bright knife; who taught
you patience as their lips fumbled to force into
sounds strange squiggles blurring on the page;
who taught you guile as the hand teases the eye

into illusion; who gave you the names you really
use for the parts of your body, for the rush
of your anger hard into your teeth and fists;
always what formed you will come trailing guilt
like a cloud of fine ashes from burnt hair.

You will always be struck into memory like a match
spurting and then burn out in silence, because
there is no one to say, yes, I too remember,
I know how it was. We litter our past
on the sides of roads in fast food wrappers.

2. Soft coal country

We used to drive to Ebensburg in the soft coal
country of Pennsylvania, an old brick Victorian
on the bottom of High Street where trucks shifted gears
to start their descent or labored upward all night;
from the backbone of High the ribs of side streets
like a fish carcass fell sharply away into gullies.
Around it were the miners' towns it served,
the grim company towns with the made-up names, Revloc,
Colver; the miners' shanties clinging to the sides
of hogback ridges, Nantiglo, Monday's Corners.

All the roads were blasted through rock.
On Horseshoe Curve you could watch the long long
freights toiling up and shrieking down, miles
around the crescent. The mountains had an anger
in them. The stone oozed bright water stained
with iron. I muttered the names of towns like prayers
returning with my father because a man must visit
his family. This was a place he had to leave,
so afraid of ending up with all grandmother's Lloyds
grubbing in the mines that when they shone
their sweet smiles at weddings, funerals, he'd
pretend he could not tell cousin from cousin.

Later when the mines shut and all the first
and second cousins were out of work for the fifth
year running and their families cracking along

old troubles, where they'd been glued, he said,
See, you can't make an honest living here.

I loved the mountains; he merely conquered them.
He returned not to see but to be seen, wearing
his one good suit, driving his nearly new car,
showing off the sexy black-haired wife not like any
in his high school yearbook, although they all knew
to sniff and say, Jew. Always the morning we left
he was up an hour early, tapping his foot under
the table, lighting cigarette from half-smoked butt
and then he would stomp his foot on the accelerator
and take the mountain roads clocking himself against
some pursuing maw so that if he did not push the car
and himself to the edge of danger, he would be back,
back with his desperate nagging sisters counting pennies
with a mountain on his chest pinning him down.

3. When I was caddy

Cleveland was the promised land of my childhood,
where my bubba cooked kosher and even her cat had good
manners and sat at the table, and she told me that
when they were alone, he used a knife and fork.
I always hoped he would do it while I was eating.

I remember the smell of the women when I pressed
against her side behind the mehitzah, camphor,

eucalyptus, cinnamon, lavender, sweat. Aunt Ruth
was the smartest girl, closer in age to me
than to my mother. When I was ten she married

into the middle class and took Bubba to the suburbs.
She worked for the Navy. What a pity you don't
have a degree, they were always telling her,
but she did the work without a rating. Driven
to excel, she began to replace all the bowling

trophies with golfing trophies. We walked to
the course through the flat green morning swishing
with sprinklers, both of us almost tiptoeing. It was
so clean and neat, the streets like a funeral parlor
full of gladiolus, we tried to talk softly, properly.

All grandma's cronies were back in the ghetto.
There was no synagogue for miles. No kosher butcher.
She ate a lot of canned salmon and packaged soup.
Without neighbors to gossip about important things
she turned to the soaps and worried about Helen Trent.

Suddenly my mother was taking phone calls at one a.m.
She was warning, Do you want to lose it all?
So he hit you. So what else is new to wives?
Then Bubba and Ruth were back in the ghetto,
now partly Black, and Bubba was cooking again.

The kitchen smelled the way it should and so did she.
Old ladies were drinking tea in glasses and quoting

Lenin and their rabbis. Every strike was fought over.
Every young woman's reputation was put through a sieve.
Every grandchild was taken and properly raised.

And me, I was back, oh briefly, briefly back
in the promised land of love and endless stories
before cancer ate Bubba, savoring each organ
but leaving her voice till the end. And Aunt Ruth
ran till she came to the Pacific and then fell down.

4. Toward a good rooting medium

The Ogibwa said to me, My people have lived
on this sea since the mountains moved.
(The last ice age.) Our heart is here.
When we move to the cities, we blow into dust.

There are villages in Cornwall
continuously occupied for five thousand years.
Jericho has been a city since 7000 B.C.E.
I've known families who farmed their soil

and gave their bones to it till it was as known
to them as the face of a mother or the body
of one passionately loved; people who have come back
to the same place year after year, and retired on it,

walking its seasons till they can read the sky
like a personal letter; fishermen who could taste

a stream and tell you what the trout were doing.
This is not a pastoral: once I loved Manhattan so.

A friend could walk Paris streets on a map, sketching
the precise light, the houses, the traffic sounds.
Perhaps we should practice by loving a lilac bush.
Practice on a brick, an oriole nest, a tire of petunias.

O home over the expressway under a sky like something
you step in and scrape off your boot, heaped
ashtray we are stubbed into with smouldering butts,
billboards touting cancer under the carbolic rain!

Will the Lenni-Lenape take back New Jersey?
The fish glow in the dark thrashing in dying
piles on every chenille bedspread, a light by which
we can almost read the fine print on the ceiling.

Love it because you can't leave it. Love it
or kill it. What we throw away returns in the blood
and leaves a chemical stain on the cell walls.
Huck honey, there's no territory to light out to.

That glow is from refineries on the farther shore.
Take your trash out with you or hunker down.
This is the Last Chance Saloon and Health Spa.
In heaven as on earth the dishes must be done.

ORANGE

The ex in the supermarket

I see him among the breakfast foods
reading labels with a dissatisfied air.
He looks softened, blurred, as if his body
had been left underwater too long.

I reach for that old pain and find it
discrete, anonymous, mildly bitter
as aspirin. It dissolves in my blood
as I try to taste it, leaving a chemical burn.

The first severed year, I avoided him
like an open pit of acid that could peel
the flesh from the skeleton of my pain.
Each bone would squeal, disjointed, red.

Now I could walk through him like smoke
and only sneeze. The pain has dispersed
into its atoms. Yet in each tiny ball
is encoded its immense violent energy.

Memory explodes of itself, cracked by a scent
of mayflower, of hot rubber, of cumin.
The past ignites in banal words of a pop song,
burning the walls of the present into gas.

I cannot walk the dog of the past at my
convenience. When memory howls gnashing
at the rusty moon, it does not even sniff at
that man pondering the peanut butter of his choice.

True romance

In a room with a nylon carpet and a daybed
a woman is dancing with her eyes on the TV set.
The face of the singer gluts. For her
he is singing, this face more familiar
than any lover's, this man she has carried
wrapped like a chocolate in the crisp paper
of her heart since she was fifteen.

She loves him, she loves him, for him
she dances, thrusting her hips, arms reaching,
churning her mons at his face bigger than
the face of her husband and closer,
more real than the smell of her own sweat.

O sunbright hero whose strut is paid for
by Japanese cars, by computers, by lite beer.
O lithe bodies the camera fills with buttercream
of wishes, bodies thin and flawless as blank paper,
bodies with nipples and navels taped, bodies
on which the clothes are glued, faces coated
with polyurethane, how many men paw at their
wives' flesh trying to unearth your vinyl.

Things move fast in that bright world. A man
sees a woman across a room and she smiles

only at him. After a diet soda commercial,
she is in bed with him. In the next scene
she is gone and his buddy the talking dog
goes at his side. Then the cars chase each other
off cliffs into balls of flame. The hero
steps out with a grin promising he will unzip
you, walk into the set of your head, turn up
the brightness and volume control till you
become real too, as the box glued to your eyes.

Yearning to repossess the body

Fever makes me luminous, a firefly.
In the night my heart throbs its strobe.
My flesh is sizzling into parchment.
Steam hangs under the ceilings, steam
that was my blood before it boiled.

Outside the oaks are cracking their knuckles
over the roof. The pines are rubbing
needles together dryly with the sound
of a brook running, so I dream of rain
while the moon hangs perfectly still

a fish eye unwinking, moments
coagulated. Then time twitches loose
and the moon skips like a single
tossed die among the wrecked boat ribs
of the sky where sail clouds rip.

Circling my fever, I wax and wane, my mind
darkens into my flu. Then I rise
from my prone body skinny as a nail
clipping and bob against the ceiling.
Down there my body quakes its bog.

I want to stuff myself like a feather
pillow back into my body's coverlet.
I want to be stitched back into the body
soundly, dance with my heavy feet.
Enough of flying on the white wind of fever!

Peeled after flu

After fever raged through both our bodies
like a brush fire out of control, the casual
strength we take for granted is combusted into wet
wood ashes, twigs charred to shattering.

An apple is a task, an adventure to conquer.
Yet warm milk fills the mouth like a benign
sweet lake of peace and plenty, the breast
world-vast once again between the lips.

We creep together fitting our bodies, a jig
saw puzzle for very young children, large
clumsy pieces we push into each other.
Pleasure blinds and stuns us into sleep.

We wake stronger, faster, harder. Already
we forget to be amazed at walking over the soft
resistant belly of the grasses. We begin to
gulp down the sun at dawn without tasting it.

A line of dancers through time

Sometimes when I'm dancing and the music
puts me on as the wind tries out a sail
I muse on heredity. They didn't go in
for words. I'm an aberration.

My Aunt Rose was dancing for the troops
in World War II, and that pension from entering
a combat zone was what she lived on
till ninety-six. She had danced for Ziegfeld,

George White's Scandals, twirled
in thirties films in costumes I was given
for Halloween. She was ten years older
than this century and still a great letter

writer till her heart stopped in her bath,
mourned by her loving younger husband.

Before her my great uncle Peter danced ballet.
About him it was said he would rather dance
than talk politics—this was not a compliment.
When my Grandfather and Great Uncle Sam

went underground, Peter still danced at the Kirov
—then the Mariinsky—pretending he wasn't a Jew
for the love of that hard use of his body,
the leaps sustained on the music,

the hover of a kestrel beating in place
before it stoops on its small prey.

Therefore in poetry I see the poem
inscribed upon time a beat, a step at a time.
I feel the poem dance me as its rhythms cohere
in the blood, on the nerves, in the organ

pipes of the bones resonating, in the trap drums
of the spine vibrating to those leaps of the mind
etched upon imaginary air, that inner space
where minute galaxies spin and pulsate

toward implosion or explosion
beads of fiercely burning ecstatically combusting
light, the only source of heat
in the absolute zero of despairing silence.

Dance is a form of trust in the body
betrayed all too soon into memory.

Heel should not be an insult

The true humility of heels:
pale, battered, wrinkled, swollen.
We may paint our toes, but naked
heels are dumb as cows' behinds.

Patient, stubborn, vulnerable
they follow us looking back
like children in cars making faces
through the rear view window.

In undressing a lover, even
foot fetishists must blink:
the sock, the stocking peeled,
the unappetizing bony fruit.

We are always landing on them
slamming them into pavement,
jumping out of trucks, forcing
them into stirrups and pedals.

Cats walk on their toes like ballerinas
but we, ape cousins, go shuffling
and what we leave in the sand
is the imprint of our heels coming home.

They are the periods under the leaping
exclamation point, gravity's mooring,

our anchor to earth, the callused
blind familiar of soil, rock, root.

Let me rub your angular barnacled
hull with unguents and massage you
tenderly, my little flatiron shaped
heroes, my hard laboring heels.

Old shoes

Old shoes, you tilt toward different poles.
Heels worn crooked. You have been
forgotten in the back of the closet
like unpunished minor crimes. This one
cheated on a test. That one lied
to get out of driving a friend
to the airport.

A bloom of bluegreen mold
greases your horsy sides.
You are prize cheeses.
Shoes, you sag like humble mouths
of beggars, shameless in displaying
your innards cracked with spent sweat.
You smell like the old dog's blanket.

Once you were bright and shapely dancers,
polished mirrors of desire: you gave me
blisters. Reluctantly I slip into you,
damp as drowned frogs. Now you slither
round me, two ancient perfect lovers.
I walk off in you, a lost habit
returned, ugliness as pure joy.

It ain't heavy, it's my purse

We have marsupial instincts, women
who lug purses as big as garbage igloos,
women who hang leather hippos from their shoulders:

we are hiding the helpless greedy naked worms
of our intentions shivering in chaos.
In bags the size of Manhattan studio apartments,

we carry not merely the apparatus of neatness
and legality, cards, licenses, combs,
mirrors, spare glasses, lens fluid,

but hex signs against disaster and loss.
Antihistamines—if we should sneeze.
Painkillers—suppose the back goes out.

Snake bite medicine—a copperhead
may lurk in the next subway car.
Extra shoes—I may have to ford a stream.

On my keyring, flats I used to stay in,
a Volvo I traded in 1985, two unknown doors
opening on what I might sometime direly need.

Ten pens, because the ink may run out.
Band-Aids, safety pins, rubber bands, glue,
maps, a notebook in case, addresses of friends

estranged. So we go hopping lopsided, women
like kangaroos with huge purses bearing hidden
our own helplessness and its fancied cures.

In June all things wake fully

The multiflora is blooming—wild roses
used before the invention of barbed wire
to fence cows from the road and the corn:
now it climbs oak trees and locusts,
sleeping beauty brambles rococo, dense,
impenetrable except by mockingbirds, robins
and the lithe black snake flashing and gone.

Ten thousand white roses quiver, flushing
the air with their perfume thick as honey.
The locusts that masquerade half the year
as woody contorted skeletons writhing,
drip with airy lemon green leaves like little
coins of light, long panicles of creamy
blossom: all locusts are candelabra gleaming.

This is the June sun that goes straight
to the spine and lights it like a taper
at the top so that the mind shines with
clean soft heat. The moving air chimes
within us. Now we want love to uncoil
feathered and slithering with blood
hotter than ours and devour us whole.

Detroit, summer camp

In Midwestern cities, behind the bungalows,
the apartment houses, the low rows of stores
run secretive thoroughfares, rats' boulevards.

In childhood I owned the alleys. Adults?
Only garbage men once a week shouting
and clanging, the junk man on his horse-drawn

wagon, gaunt hoboes drifting from the tracks.
The view over the alley fence of houses
was intimate, odorous: supper, garbage

rotting, an orange cat quick through a fence,
a hound dog tethered in a little cracked mud yard,
laundry flapping between poles, penned baby.

Boys unzipped their pants, wheedling.
Rats stood their ground flashing their teeth.
We pissed squatting behind metal igloos.

The back walls of garages were billboards
ready to be painted with obscenities, boasts,
hearts, gang graffiti: The Lords of Livernois.

There we held muttered seminars in the meaning

of power words. There we searched neighbors'
trash for whatever was only slightly broken.

It was the underside of neighbors' lives
we glimpsed, back where stories unravelled.
This was summer camp where we built bonfires,

started gasping our way to lung cancer,
learned to fight dirty and quick, tasted
our first tongues and first moonshine, twisted.

Hot, hotter

The world is a womb, hot and wet
and laboring to be delivered of August,
panting, gasping in the fever of afternoon,
sizzling night sweats and poached mornings.

Yet sweat only eases our bodies together,
oils us so we slide and skid bellies,
the bed a griddle where we hop, droplets
of ignited blood, minute's torches.

Waters flow over waters, currents melding.
Up from the rippled bottom an elbow juts,
a cockfish hunts the coral maze,
an anemone opens its fringed waving petals.

Heat asks for nakedness and nakedness
breeds inner heat releasing itself in friction.
So we make each other hotter and then cooler.
In the sticky knot of sheets we close in sleep.

The possession

The first bud of morning opens at home,
September first, a clean salty wind scouring
the air of exhaust and dust. Lumbering in
on the dowager DC-3 I could see the storm signs
in the barred sunset last night. Now at mid
morning, the clouds are bleaching to gauze,
tearing. The leaves are brighter. Pools
stand at low points in the blacktop.

The first good sleep in a week, cradled
in my own bed with the right sounds of dogwood
soughing, creaking, wind in the TV antennae
and the pines, I am peeled of dry husks.
My skin drinks light. I come home to a pump
that dies six times a day, losing all pressure;
a boundary dispute; a nonfiction tome of bills
to read and pay, a disordered epic of mail.

I used to drift past houses, wistful and contemptuous.
A creature of the night, I felt free
of those bonds of drapery and appliance cord.
I was formed of sharp hungers simple as knives
and they drove me or let me drop into ennui,
yet I saw all houses as bourgeois mousetraps

whose cheese I was too cagey to taste no matter
how many cold miles I might chase my supper.

I lived in eight cities building my chancy
nests high and low, able to set up temporary
housekeeping in a closet, abandoning used sofas
and tables as a hermit crab switches found shells.
Yet when I came here, I metamorphosed.
I grew down into this hill, tap-rooted deep.
I am made now out of water from this well
blood and tissue and bone. This land owns me.

Persimmon pudding

Smooth, lacquered you shine like a Japanese box.
Your color is enamel flame.
To bite into you then is to twist the mouth
round an acid roar, to pucker on a kiss
that flays the tongue, scrapes the palate raw.

We must wait while perfection slides by,
till your skin wrinkles, till its gloss dims.
Then, only then you open in the mouth
a lively mellow alto sax sweetness,
rich as amber, creamy on the tongue.

You counsel patience, attunement with the seasons
and each act come to its fullness of time.
But mostly, O vermillion, you suggest a metaphor
for a woman a bit past ripe but sweeter
she swears for the touch of frost.

Shad blow

1.

Deer tracks cloven dark in the pale sand.
The grey squirrels shriek and chase each other
crashing from branch to branch of the oaks.

The shad bloom is late this year and perfect,
trees that are one great composite flower,
wild carrots, Queen Anne's Lace the size

of giraffes riffled by the breeze
miles of salt have scrubbed
bone white. Orange and lemon orioles

flit among knotted branches. The trunks
of shad are grey, blotched with lichen,
fog caught and woven into wood.

2.

I used to lie under the sour cherry in the narrow
yard of the house where we moved the year
I turned fifteen. White galaxies that would become

wine by summer's end, pies in the sky,
flashed against the sulfurous clouds of Detroit—
blossoms out of mahogany bark shining.

Who will I be? The will to love

ate holes in my mind. I was riddled
like a sieve with sharp sour desires.

I can taste that raw homemade wine,
taste a sweet and sour intoxicating pain
so empty, wanting played shrilly on me

like the wind over the mouth of a bottle
compelling a keening too high pitched
for a human to notice, but the dog next

door flung back his head and howled too
and my cat came stepping through the unmown
grass to circle three times, then marked

the tree with his spray as I burned
to mark the world with something of mine.
Spring came on like cramps in a growing body.

3.

In spring I raise my head to sniff at scents.
I want to be out by the river watching the ale
wives straddling the current, humping upstream.

I thrust my hands into the cool rich soil,
the moss like fur between the cracks of the stones.
I want to roll like a big dog and shake free.

The salamander cool as jelly, darkly colored

as cabernet sauvignon lies on my palm
then leaps to freedom, snap, in the wood pile.

Appetite licks at the air, the tiny leaves
opening their clenched silken banners.
At two in the afternoon the fox runs on the beach

going to paw at the late alewives crossing
the bar where the brook eases into the bay.
A gull runs at him, then flaps off.

Once I thought the seasons were mine,
moods, passions, itches I could scratch,
voids I could fill with other's bodies.

Now I know I am in the seasons, of them.
The sun warms the upturned soil and my arm.
Spring moves through me like an armada of light.

YELLOW

Bite into the onion

Take a big bite and let its jagged fumes pierce
the roof of your mouth and kick your sinuses.
All the fine layers of it intricate as a mosaic,
wrapped like a present, in wine colored silk of the red,
the plain brown wrapper of the pornographic yellow
that will strip and strip for you down to the baby core,
the ivory parchment of the white.

Everyone all day will know what you had for lunch.
They will back off from you with a look of polite
distaste and stand across the room barking like poodles.
You will sneak up on your friends and give them a big
kiss of hostility and affection mixed in a busy palette.
Your own breath will hang around you in a prickly
holly wreath hung with its own internal bells.

Onion, I undress you in your wardrobe of veils,
I enter you room upon room inside each other
like Russian dolls. You sizzle in my nose,
healthy, obstinate, loud as a peasant uncle
coming in with his boots dirty and a chicken
with its neck wrung clutched in his fist.
What soup or stew is not empty without you?

Cooked, you change your whole character.
You are suave and unctuous, polite to mushrooms

and the palest fish. You play under the meal
like a well-bred string quartet in a posh restaurant,
pianissimo, legato, just enough to mute cutlery.
You are the ideal lover for every entree.
Animal or vegetable, you tickle them all.

Your cousins are my darlings, the leek—a scallion
taking steroids, the sly magenta shallots, the garlic
that blesses food, the Egyptian onions that go down on
their knees to plant themselves. But many times
nothing but you will do, big as a wrestler's fist,
obvious as a splash of yellow paint in the roadway,
when food must slam a door, roar and shout.

Toward a sudden silence

The vast dry sand dunes are stirring.
The wind is blowing them so they choke
trees struggling to grow above the smothering
creep. The wind is blowing them so they bury
houses and collapse the walls inward, crushed.

The wind is sandblasting my windshield
so I cannot see where I am speeding
with my foot stomped to the floor.
The wind is blinding me with my own tears
as I stumble one step at a time into dust.

My steps are brushed out as I push forward.
I could be walking in place. I could be
rushing in wide or narrowing circles.
This sand gets into the mouth, its grit
grinding on the teeth. This sand invades

the water canteen, crawls between the hairs
to the scalp. It slips into the seams of clothes.
Only sometimes the wind falls and I can see
with a clarity that aligns the mind and the spine
where I have been, where I can still try to go.

The heart's clock

Through the darkness the house paddles
oars of light splashing through the trees.
In the plain of dazzling white sand, the house
curls around its darkness, eyes shut tight.

Strings of patio lights, floods mounted under
the eaves, porch lights, wan colonizers all.

Sunlight breaks around the block of house,
leaking through the windows, slipping in cracks,
dashing its foam over the slate shingles
while the rock heart slumbers on in its chill.

We rip out the belly of the woods to put up
these wooden caves in which we crouch
in darkened rooms watching boxes of dim color
flash images captured under studio lights.

Making our own day and night we tick
like crazed watches our own eccentric time.

We can live without ever watching the sun
rise, the moon set and swell and shrink,
without knowing our own sunflower organs turn
through the hours of light toward their source.

The truth according to Ludd

The pleasure of kicking the vacuum cleaner
is irrational, yes, for it has no nerves
but is it more rational to kick the dog
when the cappuccino maker blows its lid?

Who is to blame when the washing machine
turns into a gusher? When the answering
machine drones your message from under water?
When the electrical system on your car

goes at midnight in January up on Killer
Mountain or in the fast lane on the expressway
at five fifteen? Machines flash us their idiot
plastic grins but we know that inside

something that turns the crank can go on strike.
Demons live in electricity as eels in water
lurking, equally happy to drink our blood
or simply curdle the milk and fry our hair.

When the computer prints for the sixteenth straight
time Bad Command or Can't Find That File
you know it is laughing silently inside,
like the car whose secret motto is Born to Cough.

We imagine they are extensions to our bodies,
sleek, perfect. Our egos preen in them.
Machines do not love us as we love them.
They have the contempt the whore does for johns.

Getting it back

When the guests have gone, the house is twice
as big. Quiet blows through it like silver
light that touches every chair and plate
to the precision of objects in a Vermeer.

We face each other and slowly begin to talk,
not making conversation as one plans and then
cooks a company dinner, but improvising,
the words spiraling up and out in a dance

as intricate and instinctual as the choral
wave of the swallows darting on the silken
twilight pale as a moon snail shell, till between
us the hanging nest of our intimacy is rewoven.

Domestic danger

You are my best miracle. Above
the answering machine, the copier
and the dryer, we float on gyres of noise
like blown paper. Then the dust storm
of the mind stills to clarity and I
can see your eyes.

Balanced on the blade of a fan
churning the air, we entwine.
All things chop at us
but we hover together
where we would separately fall.
In chaos we dance.

In this dance no one leads,
although we both push, pull
on the other's stubborn momentum
and inertia, trying to put
our own spin on this mutual
orbit hurtling through space.

Easy to forget the shock
of the miracle and turn love
into a background hum, air
conditioning, the hiss on a record,
when it is the electricity
that powers us.

When too much is barely enough

The scent of butter and cream honeysuckle
is ladled like sambuca straight into my brain;
wild roses tumble among tawny grasses.

After a cool spring water-soaked and walled in,
fog like packing material propping the trees,
leaves that lengthen slowly as hair grows,

slugs nibbling the cabbage to wet lace,
the ground squishing underfoot and a smell
of drains, the sky a toadstool,

July is a brass fanfare danced by a pride
of lions. The wind is a blue circus tent
flapping in great rolling billows of light.

The sun paints my lids vermillion.
The sun lays its red paw on my belly and thighs.
The sun stands on my head crowing.

The road is paved with soft licorice.
The ocean is turtle soup, winy with seaweed.
The moon drops down at night till it floats

just over the pines and the owl sits on it.
Rabbits dash everywhere in the fields and roads,
grass with legs and white blossoms.

Under me the sand heaves and sighs.
The air is ripe and perfumed as a peach.
Who could eat this day and not be filled?

Frog song

Water lilies float like half moons
on Herring Pond silent as marble
where ragged and patchy alewives
drag themselves along in the spring
and finally home free, spawn.

We paddle our canoe swishing on flat
landing pads. The cups of the lilies
rise, dreams almost taking off
but held on their long balloon
strings anchored in fishy muck.

The canoe glides over dream lilies.
Oh havoc, oh crushing waste. But they
pop up behind us with drops of water
glittering. Translucent alewife
minnows quiver under them, hiding.

We slide over sky caught flashing
among pads. We loll on the outstretched
palm of summer. A dragonfly scouts us,
zips off while the sun leaves the gold
smear of its thumb on every sigh.

Yellow, red, blue

The sun melts through the body and turns it to joy.
The sea breathes heavily. How shaggy and plumed
the breakers twist whitening the distance.
The air shines with salt and minute droplets.

The sea is slowing. My pulse is sinking
below the horizon where cobalt takes turquoise,
the smoke of a ship dwindling off the world.
Voices shimmer and fade. Tensions squawk once

and then grow heavy and drown in limpidity.
My names evaporate. I am flesh like hot stone.
Cook an egg on me, I won't mind more than
asphalt does. I am smoked and salted away.

Words wheel up like a flight of sandpipers
and flash off. Sand scours me simple.
Rub my belly, I purr; kick sand, I bark.
Otherwise I'm empty as a perfect whelk shell.

Woman in the bushes

A snail easing gingerly
tasting the morning's dangers with soft
gelatinous eyestalks probing
each direction, she shuffles forward,
her only house her back bearing
all the clothing remaining to her
and her shopping cart
piled with her blanket roll,
her Sterno, pan and bottle,
her photographs wilted like flowers.

This fall she sleeps in a rhodo-
dendron thicket in the park,
withdrawing deep among the leathery
leaves when twilight makes of grass
a minefield of exploding boys.

While the joggers prance past,
the cyclists in neon gear,
she wriggles out, washes
at a fountain, fills her bottle.
In the hollow among oaks shedding
she squats where the police
cannot see and heats beans.

Nothing human separates
us like comfort.
Suburban housewife, secretary,
nurse, writer, mother of six,

can you trot by without
feeling yourself ghostly slipping
into her pile of unwashed sweaters,
her grey shivering skin.

A local doctor describes a body dead
of exposure last winter: multiparous,
more than one child delivered.
Her teeth revealed a life once affluent.
Hunger sucked her like a spider.
Marks of severe malnutrition, he said,
frostbite.

We despise what isn't new. We toss
half of what we buy. Things are made
to break and we discard them. Excess
people take longer to get rid of
but they biodegrade nicely.
It just takes time and weather.

Blizzard comes

Snow clings in circles to the side of the trees
crooked saddles for the wind to mount.
Grins along every twig.

Snow slices crossways through the air,
each particle hard, shining.
The wind is serrated.

My youngest cat cries at the window,
trying to attract that snow's attention:
the storm is a huge animal,

a white wind beast snorting and stamping.
The umbilical cord of the mail is cut.
The p.o. is dark as Sunday.

Now we are truly perched on an island,
the highway trackless, the bridges glazed with ice,
storm tides surging over low roads

and the snow coming on as I play with my hair
wishing I could crawl into its cave and sleep,
wishing I could ride the wind, a sail

tearing loose and billowing out over the foaming
sea that is trackless as the land now,

roads buried and houses sticking up like blisters.

Only the fine spun net of electricity
binds us to our postindustrial now.
When the lights go out, we are sullen as bears

and have only a stove, our stock of chopped
trees, a comforter and each other's flesh
to warm us in the vortex of whirling ice.

A newly sharpened wind

The ground is a sponge full of the brown water
the snow has become. It trickles deep,
slowly melting the hard pan of winter,
easing down through the filters of earth
and gravel to arrive pristine as sand
sliding into the precious water table.

We squish as we walk. Soil clumps
in my fist, as every day I grab a handful
waiting for the day it crumbles like cake
and we start tucking the seeds in furrows.
Where the hunters pursued the panicked deer
and blood stained the fawn colored grass

dark as tar, the water creeps and spills.
Every dip is a pond calling to the geese
beating over; every gully and rut is a fresh
stream wriggling, contours of the land
silvered by the moon rising on the marsh.
At night strange ducks squat in the pines.

On the plainsong bones of the winter trees
buds are swelling into polyphonic motions,
baroque architecture of soar and shimmer.
The seals bark. Where are the whales of spring?
Tides of migration wake me at dawn restless
to be out stirred by the sharp scented wind.

For each age, its amulet

Each illness has its demon, burning you with
its fever, beating its quick wings.
Do not leave an infant alone in the house,
my grandmother said, for Lilith is hovering,
hungry. Avoid sleeping in a new house alone.
Demons come to death as flies do, hanging
on the sour sweetish wind. Protect yourself
in an unclean place by spitting three times.
A pregnant woman must go to bed with a knife.
Put iron in a hen's nest to keep it laying.
Demons suck eggs and squeeze the breath from chicks.
Circle yourself with salt and pray.

By building containers of plutonium
with the power to kill for longer than humans
have walked upright, demons are driven off.
Demons lurk in dark skins, white skins,
demons speak another language, have funny hair.
Very fast planes that fall from the sky
regularly like ostriches trying to fly, protect.
Best of all is the burning of money ritually
in the pentagon shaped shrine. In Langley
the largest prayer wheel computer recites spells
composed of all words written, spoken, thought
taped and stolen from every living person.

Returning to the cemetery in the old Prague ghetto

Like bad teeth jammed crooked in a mouth
I think, no, because it goes on and on,
rippling among uneven hillocks among the linden
trees drooping, their papery leaves piling
up in the narrow paths that thread
between the crowded tilting slabs.

Stone pages the wind blew open.
The wind petrified into individual
cries. Prisoners penned together
with barely room to stand upright.
Souls of the dead Jews of Prague
waiting for justice under the acid rain.

So much and no further shall you go,
your contaminated dead confined between
strait walls like the ghetto itself.
So what to do? Every couple of generations,
pile on the dirt, raise the stones up
and add another layer of fresh bones.

The image I circle and do not want:
naked pallid bodies whipped through
the snow and driven into the chamber,
so crowded that dying slowly in the poison
cloud they could not fall as their nerves
burned slowly black, upright in death.

In my luggage I carried from Newcomb Hollow
two stones for Rabbi Loew's memorial
shaped like a narrow tent, one for Judah

on his side and one for Perl on hers.
But my real gift is the novel they
speak through. For David Gans, astronomer,

geographer, historian, insatiably curious
and neat as a cat in his queries,
I brought a fossil to lay at the foot
of his grave marked with a goose and a star,
Mogen David, so the illiterate could find
him, as Judah has his rampant lion.

In sixty-eight I had to be hoisted
over the fence. Among the stones
I was alone except for a stray black cat
that sang to me incessantly of need,
so hungry it ate bread from my jacket pocket.
This year buses belch out German tourists

and the graves are well tended.
This is a place history clutches you
by the foot as you walk the human earth,
like a hand grabbing from the grave,
not to frighten but to admonish.
Remember. History is the iron

in your blood carrying oxygen
so you can burn food and live.
Read this carved book with your fingers
and your failing eyes. The language
will speak in you silently
nights afterward, stone and bone.

GREEN

I have always been poor at flirting

I know it's harmless. My friends who flirt
the hardest—consummate, compulsive—are least
apt to fall into bed on a hot night's wind.
Flirting is what they do instead of sex,
five-year affairs of eyes and telephone trysts
voices soft as warm taffy, artful laughs,
a hush when the spouse walks through the room.

Yet when I flirt I feel like an elephant
in a pink tutu balancing on a beach ball,
a tabby wearing a doll's dress, stuffed
in a carriage, about to snarl and slash.
I am pretending to be a girl, a girly girl.
A smile hangs on my face like a loose shutter.
My voice is petroleum jelly on my tongue.

My mother flirted with the milkman, the iceman,
the butcher—oh he winked and strutted,
flashing his gold tooth and slapping the scale.
Ogling, the plumber fixed both leaks
for the price of one. She flirted with the mailman,
the paperboy who brought our paper and only ours
to the door. I'd watch sour as a rotten lemon,

dour as a grandfather clock, cringing, muttering
Mother! like the curse word it was. The walls
would drip perfumed oil. The ceiling sagged buttery.
Her eyes were screwed wide open, Betty Boop,
batting butterfly wings, her mouth pursed,
while she played them like saxophones,
her voice now a tiny plush mouse,

now sleeking into the lower registers

of dark honey lapping at the belly.
When we couldn't pay the mortgage, she almost
climbed into the bank manager's lap.
Motorcycle cops pulling over our sputtering car,
teachers, principals, my father's bosses,
she had only one weapon, shameless silent

promises redeemable for absolutely nothing
but an ego job on the spot, frothing over.
If afterward she called them behayma,
fool, it was with quiet satisfaction,
an athlete who has performed well and won.
I remember the puzzled damaged look in her
widened eyes when flirting began to fail.

For some it is a drug of choice,
a moment's cocaine spiking the ego, giving
that spurt of a mirror cooing attraction.
For me it means only, I am powerless,
you can hurt or help me, wedged there above,
so I attempt this awkward dance of the broken
fan and the mud colored bubble, among your teeth.

Attraction to me is a walking toward,
the doors in the hands and the mind slowly
swinging on their hinges so that something
can pass over and something new enter.
This flicking of the body like a cape before
a bull, this mincing of the hook under the
feathers is more war and less love than I need.

The diminishing addition

It's a madness that comes over us every seven
years, whenever we might lay money by.
Instead we are contemplating our tiny kitchen,
frowning at a dark stuffy scruffy bedroom
and the urge strikes: Imagine a window there,
a sun room, a porch, a bathroom: an extension.

The key word is tension. The desire to call
a wrecking crew into our lives, to rip a large
hole in the walls and let chaos in,
to sieve the fabric of existence to the chug
of cement mixers and the banging of hammers
and the roar of ghetto blasters tuned

to stations we hate. Oh, why can't we
resist? Snort it up the nose, stick
it in our arm, drink it by the gallon,
throw a large party and invite the Marines
and the local high school, just start
a fire and barbecue a rat over the coals

of banked up dollars. But no, the fantasies
of more living room drive us as mad
as Hitler, only we are weak, foolish Poland
invaded by mechanized armies wielding

power tools, defended by a cavalry of cats.
I'm moving underground, burrowing blind

and paddle-footed toward velvet silence.
An addition is first a subtraction, then
a division with walls that crumble like bad
fillings, ceilings that leak like the economy,
carpenters who swear they will finish tomorrow
then take a Caribbean cruise, electricians

harder to capture than Bigfoot, plumbers
whose bills would bankrupt the Pentagon.
But it's like childbirth. The results erase
the process and you can't remember a before.
The new room floats in light. The kitchen glitters.
You start envisioning a second story.

Practicing with the windows open

Inside she is chained to the piano
while neighborhood kids peddle past on bikes,
roar past on roller skates, play stickball
in loud voices breaking like wine glasses.

She plays scales, does exercises for strengthening
the fourth finger of the left hand. Then
she opens her music. Soon thousands of azure
butterflies in Brownian movement claim the street.

Now they are white. Now they are tiger moths
fluttering through windows. Nobody can think
of anything but Mozart. She has scrubbed every skull
on the block and filled each with fresh flowers.

Little Pischna revisited

Every workshop I teach, he or she sweeps in,
sits at the back with a sly smile, as if to say
I float above you peasants like a silk kite.

Student conferences are dental appointments
without anesthesia where we try to pull
each other's teeth with our fingernails.

I know what she wants, simply to be anointed
and let into the room where the anthem shakes
the air like stage thunder and mouths say O.

I have been there too, that arrogant wishful
waltz with a phantom. Music was my early folly.
I wanted to sit down at the piano and rumble

rainbow arpeggios. I wanted to slip into Chopin
like a satin negligee, but the notes were black
mazes of thorns that trapped my fingers.

What I got was Mr. McGillis, ironic red
eyed bachelor with his head conical,
leathery as a football, but freckled,

his huge hands, his teeth grinding in pain.
I wanted to play with feeling and the pedal,

blurring I hoped my constant goofs and almosts.

He set me to the Little Pischna, exercises,
boredom. "The fourth finger is weak, lazy."
He would glare, pulling it like a teat.

"You have the discipline of a wet towel."
Music was a warm bath where I floated in love,
music was my drug of choice at age nine.

My seventeenth summer, when I set myself
to work through Bartók's *Mikrokosmos*
I remembered that gnarled walking stick of man

with a new respect. Poetasters, gushers,
the adolescent of all ages who finger
their own words reverently as rosary beads,

I am their dour mean angel with a sword
brandishing NO like a tollgate outside Paradise.
I am nasty Lavan setting them to labor seven

years for the wrong sister; but the sisters
are joined, and you can't marry one without wedding
the other in the same strait bed of the poem.

Teaching experience

Pour into them.
I am a sprinkling can dribbling.
The only rainbows I make
are painted on air.

I gather myself.
I darken with energy.
I rumble and burst
forth into torrents,
flashing electricity
in the slack pale faces.

One is cracking his knuckles,
another glares at me,
another is stoned and slumps
on the end of her spine,
the fourth is rehearsing the balcony
scene, the fifth is pricing
my clothing piece by piece.

You are used to television
that goes when you turn
it on, or video games active
to your coins. If you
put your finger in my
mouth I might suck it,

I might bite if off.

One to one I could teach,
I could learn, for every person
I have touched has made me
rich with pleasure and pain
slow deposits in memory
like shale laid down.

I could show you how
to prune a grapevine, I could
show you how to roast a goose
wasting nothing, not the bones
for soup or the fat rendered
its sweet aroma spreading.
I could show you the red eye
of Antares, I could show you
where the marsh hawk builds
her gawky nest, how to follow
through banks and paper thickets
the spore of a corporate
choice in damaged genes.

In these rooms words float
devoid of their shadows in action.
Teach poetry? Learn how

to wring the neck of a chicken,
how to sustain orgasm, learn
how to build and mend. In universities
one learns about universities,
in jail about jail. If in poetry
all you learn is words,
you pass wind.

Breath is the life.
Breathe words that move you
out, that speed your blood and slow
it, words that wake auras,
words that ignite and cause tears,
but use your hands, use
your back, use the long muscles
of your legs, use your twin
lobes of forebrain and the wise
snake coiled on your spine.
Let words be born from you
wet and kicking. Let them cry,
but you, keep quiet and moving.

For she is a tree of life

In the cramped living room of my childhood
between sagging rough-skinned sofa that made me itch
and swaybacked chair surrounded by ashtrays
where my father read every word of the paper
shrouded in blue smoke, coughing rusty phlegm
and muttering doom, the rug was a factory
oriental and the pattern called tree of life.

My mother explained as we plucked a chicken,
tree of life: I was enthralled and Hannah
my grandmother hummed for me the phrase
from liturgy: Eytz khayim hee l'makhazikim
bo v'kol nitee-voteh-ho shalom:
for she is a tree of life to all who hold her fast,
and the fruit of her branches is peace.

I see her big bosomed and tall as a maple
and in her veins the beige sugar of desire
running sometimes hard, surging skyward
and sometimes sunk down into the roots
that burrow and wriggle deep and far among rocks
and clay and the bones of rabbits and foxes
lying in the same bed at last becoming one.

I see her opening into flushed white
blossoms the bees crawl into. I see her

branches dipping under the weight of the yield,
the crimson, the yellow and russet globes,
apples fallen beneath the deer crunch.
Yellow jackets in the cobalt afternoon buzz
drunken from cracked fruit oozing juice.

We all flit through her branches or creep
through her bark, skitter over her leaves.
Yet we are the mice that gnaw at her root
who labor ceaselessly to bring her down.
When the tree falls, we will not rise as plastic
butterfly spaceships, but will starve as the skies
weep hot acid and the earth chafes into dust.

Subtle commands of the earth

All winter long the air is slightly rusted iron,
the air is salt, ice, wet wool,
the smell of fresh pine split, cherry wood,
the dark seep of decay just starting.

One morning the wind suddenly rubs against
your leg like a cat. One morning the air
trails chiffon across your nape, flirting.
Green herbs push up beside straw hulks.

Honey floats. You stop and sniff
taking a point unconsciously, a vestigial
tail straight out in the mind, the mouth
falling open as if you could still taste

a smell. The air shimmers with sweetness
that ripples through the veins like wine.
The pheromones of flowers prick us sore
till we fall on each other like starving foxes.

The 31st of March

A cold insistent rain swells the buds.
Swamp maples begin to redden, a scarlet
that taunts the corner of the eye.
Lichens swell and fur the oak boughs.
In Paradise Hollow, a mourning cloak
idles past like an animated kerchief
haunting bare branches. Look: the wood
cock rises in feathered desire.

Green uncoils pressed against earth,
grasses, moss, bulb spears pricking up,
the tiny leaves of pesky chickweed.
The first slug of spring extends itself
like a yawn across the sand. My next
year splits open to show its first color.

It arrives suddenly and
carries us off as usual

Sometimes in early June I am standing
under the just unpacked green of the oak
when a hot bearish paw suddenly flattens the air:
a warm front marches in palpable as
a shove, a sudden fanfare from the brass.

I am putting dishes away in the cupboard.
You are screwing a bulb into the fixture:
is it the verb, the analogy, the mischievous
child of the limbic brain fitting shards together?
We both think of sex as if a presence

had entered the room, a scent of salt
and hot feathers, a musky tickle
along the spine like arpeggios
galloping down the scale to the bass
that resonates from skull to soles.

The body that has been functioning,
a tidy machine, retracts its armor
of inattention and the skin shimmers
with mouths of light crying let me take
you in, I must be laved in touch.

Now, now. Five minutes later
we are upstairs, the phone out of the wall,
doors locked, clothes tossed like casualties

through three rooms. We are efficient
in our hunger, neat as a sharpshin stooping.

Half an hour after that we are back,
me at the cupboard, you on the ladder
our clothes rumpled, reeking of secretions
and satisfaction, dazed as if carried
to a height and dropped straight down.

Why I bought the
stupid palm tree dish

The woman waits at the dipping card table.
Spread before her, a chipped wooden spoon,
a pink shaded shepherdess boudoir lamp,
canning jars, clip earrings imitating pearls,
a plush white unicorn, fishing lures
with rusted hooks still lethally barbed.

On the worn grass of the yard like lame
flamingos two floor lamps huddle among
kitchen chairs, a crib. On a clothesline
she has strung her closet rejects.
Cars stop at the hand lettered sign,
come waving the local paper want ads,

early birds, dealers. It is sadness
on sale, for hope placed that cardinal
welcome mat, and the winged thing has flown.
These vessels of marriage hit the tile floor
at missile speed detonating into shards
each sharp enough to pierce a vein.

For money she is hoping to trade her past
that no longer fits, a past without use
or aesthetic appeal, pain in the guise
of out-of-style white high heeled shoes,
shaped into swan ashtrays arching their necks,
packed in a heart shaped leaking aluminum mold.

A garden of words

1.

A garden is all we will ever taste of paradise;
the green flood dammed into exquisite waterfalls,
fountains, brooks whose meanderings are artfully
structured and whose ponds reflect composed views.

The whole caresses each fragment. A prize
of bad art, Victorian copy of a poor imitation
of the Roman copy of a lost Greek original
as it kneels among the grey santolina,

orients the gaze in the maze of clipped box,
threads the needle through the sculptured yews.
Although on a hosta's blue leaf, a spider
devours a white butterfly, in paradise

spiders bloom too as willows drink the sun,
for the humus is rich with small fallen bodies.

2.

The white cat sits in the red and blue rain
of paisley-shaped drops while the red satin
throat of the hummingbird all tinsel and spark
glitters and then it is gone with a whir.

Yellow spiders in the yellow marigolds
do not spin webs but jump like great cats,

jonquil bright cheetahs from ambush.
Lemon goldfinches sing saffron arias.

The eyes of the blue geraniums open wide
veined softly. Sharp gothic spires of larkspur.
Sink into blue as into a soothing dream
of breathable water. Climb into blue

high and fierce as the wind that polishes
granite ledges where the last bright wild
flowers grow in a crack on the slab where
runoff from the glacier runs milky green.

White flowers, white gardens are the wind
caught and tamed in lace, the mockery
of snow against the sizzling fat of summer,
the coolness of shade promised in full sun.

3.

Green, green, you are the shade we can drink
and drink and never grow drunken and never
grow full. In a museum after two rooms
I have a bellyache of rich surfeit in the eyes.

But I can walk these hills and the eye will
not weary with green but swim in it buoyed up.
Green, green, you are various as an orchestra,
the small smooth leaves of cottoneaster,

the long waxy sheaves of rhododendron, blueish
spears of iris, grooved diamonds of dogwood,
bristling juniper spikes, plumes of white pine.
The gaze will strengthen itself and lengthen,

a knot in the back of the brain uncoil.
It is a serpent that slept unheeded. Now
it stands to dance and the body is loosed
from its tight bones to swirl like water.

The body falls down like rain and sinks
into the leaves and sleeps the way it had
forgotten as the shapes of leaves float
on the blood, boats ferrying silence.

4.

I will build a walled garden under the sun.
In it I will plant the useful herbs homely
and sweet scented, and old perennials
that mingle beauty and medicine and myth,

foxglove, valerian, yarrow, wormwood,
rose and verbena. I will tease nature

into shapes of artifice and temptation.
It will be art and jungle. In this garden

I will go to find cats sleeping wrapped around
the espaliered pear tree trunk like furry snakes.
I'll dance aimless and driven as a butterfly
pale among the cabbages I devour, savoy,

red like giant brains, myself studying
to be natural and unnatural at once.

BLUE

The Book of Ruth and Naomi

When you pick up the Tanakh and read
the Book of Ruth, it is a shock
how little it resembles memory.
It's concerned with inheritance,
lands, men's names, how women
must wiggle and wobble to live.

Yet women have kept it dear
for the beloved elder who
cherished Ruth, more friend than
daughter. Daughters leave. Ruth
brought even the baby she made
with Boaz home as a gift.

Where you go, I will go too,
your people shall be my people,
I will be a Jew for you,
for what is yours I will love
as I love you, oh Naomi
my mother, my sister, my heart.

Show me a woman who does not dream
a double, heart's twin, a sister
of the mind in whose ear she can whisper,
whose hair she can braid as her life
twists its pleasure and pain and shame.
Show me a woman who does not hide

in the locket of bone that deep
eye beam of fiercely gentle love

she had once from mother, daughter,
sister; once like a warm moon
that radiance aligned the tides
of her blood into potent order.

At the season of first fruits we recall
two travellers, co-conspirators, scavengers
making do with leftovers and mill ends,
whose friendship was stronger than fear,
stronger than hunger, who walked together
the road of shards, hands joined.

Underwater breathing

Then I went down to the river
milky and whispering as Venus winked
crescent shaped like a tiny burning moon
over the bristly pines muttering.

Then I slid into the river
like a baby snapper hatched in the parched
and blazing sand who runs with her little
legs while the gulls pick off her brothers

runs, runs to the smell of water
and then slides in, dropping,
a flat stone that meant to skip
and then suddenly the short legs

are dragging hard at the water
the right way and the turtle swims.
I went down to the river, fell in and began
to drown but then, as the waters

knocked on my head and throat,
as my chest pumped its wheezing bellows,
I remembered my ancient gills and swam
deep and far, to the red eye

in the black heart of the green
exploding roar. The secret is giving
over, the knack is the brain sliding
into the body till it can swim underblood.

Detroit means strait

Down to the river, down, down,
and in those days the old brick streets did slope
in that direction, although you could rarely
see it, broad as a plain of molten steel
gleaming briefly between foundry and factory.

When I was little and we drove in our grey Terraplane
past the giant stove on East Jefferson and under,
through the viaduct, we passed into a brilliant world
on the bridge to Belle Isle, where two hot Junes
later, the Detroit race riot started with shoving.

The river did not belong to kick the can on baking
asphalt, nor did ore boats rusty and high as buildings
nor the little craft with white sails dipping,
the girls with their sailors kissing on blankets,
the tiered fountain like a liquid wedding cake.

The other entry to that radiant magic water space
was the dock by the plant that made Vernors
which tasted of real ginger, a heady reek,
the excursion boat to Bob Lo—Bois Blanc—
an amusement park on an island where class trips went.

There when cicadas emerged, they were called
Canadian soldiers. Dried bodies lay in drifts
among the picnic tables. By that age, I knew

a boy killed at Dieppe, so the name, a joke
or insult, had a dark muddy aftertaste of pain.

Still it was a real frontier I crossed to visit
two old Spanish anarchists, house full of bright
dead magazines like fallen leaves from a tree of hope,
Emma Goldman's twenty years of letters in a suitcase
in that Windsor attic whistling for love.

Your eyes recall old fantasies

The Aegean of your eyes—remembered
spring of thirty years ago
when you were an abused, drugged child
and I dragged through Greek villages
with a man who daily polished his anger
till it shone whitely as glass
in the sun, kept it hidden,
denied, until he buried
its dagger in my flesh.

The landscape loved me instead.
The poppies shouted orgasm.
The light brushed my bones
till they glowed secretly,
cuneiform shapes in the night
of my despair, an alphabet
beginning to form that when
I returned would shape
into poems in my changing voice.

That sea was clear down to dark
sharp rocks, the shapes of ancient
wrecks; teemed with dancing octopi,
red mullet flashing like glimpses
of desire teasing me with hope.
Then the wind roused it to opaque

fury, thudding like granite
against the prow of the boat
that bore a woman's staring eye.

It was the eye of the bold
sensual woman of the Cretan wall
paintings who walked bare breasted
without fear across the goddess's
rocky lap. Your joy is too young
for you, the oracle murmured,
but I was too young to understand,
promises etched in my flesh
in a language I could not yet read.

Wet

Desire urges us on deeper
and farther into the coral maze
of the body, dense, tropical
where we cannot tell plant
from animal, mind from body
prey from predator, swaying
magenta, teal, green-golden
anemones weaving wide open.

The stronger lusts flash
corn rows of dagger teeth,
but the little desires slip,
sleek frisky neon flowers
into the corners of the eye.
The mouth tastes their strange
sweet and salty blood
burning the back of the tongue.

Deeper and deeper into
the thick warm translucence
where mind and body melt,
where we see with our tongues
and taste with our fingers;
there the horizon of excess

folds as we approach
into plains of not enough.

Now we are returned to ourselves
flung out on the beach
exhausted, flanks heaving
out of oxygen and time,
grinning like childish daubs
of boats. Now it is sleep
draws us down, surrendered
to its dark glimmer.

Three a.m. feeding

Three a.m. and I think the moon
has risen until I realize it is just baleful
lamplight with a blue watery cast.
A car flicks past like a minnow.

Down ten floors a woman is rocking
in a doorway crying. Her sobbing woke
me rising like a bird shaken from its nest
in the rough dark to beat wildly against leaves.

For a moment we are joined by her pain
as if a single arrow transfixed us.
A man then takes her by the arm and pulls
her along the street arguing his will.

Don't go with him, I want to shout
out of the hotel window at the woman who
never saw me, whose face and race are blank,
whose pain still pierces me, become my own.

Anxiety wins a round

All night stone is grinding upon stone.
Fear throbs like a dying nerve in a tooth.
Our bed is carried on swift flood waters
swirling round and round among drowned
cows and plucked roofs.
                                    I know your scent
in the dark and the warmth vibrating
from your shoulders. I know which cat
is curled against my bent knee, which
sprawls with a paw on my calf,

but though I fumble through my ribs
rummage up old costumes of memory,
I have no self, but dangerous night
presses in on my brain like a huge
icy thumb. The moment impales me.

Fear makes me simple, a lab rat lost
in a shocking maze. Dawn will give me back
my intelligence with the rising smoky sun.
I will put on my life with my clothes
and walk on the painted map called reality.

We speak of seeing the heron, as if there were only one

Dawn, the sky split by an incoming front,
half aquamarine egg, half rumpled frost clouds,
Wellfleet Bay smooth, grooved only with the wakes
of ducks, we stepped out onto the dike marching
smartly, thirty degrees, clear and still,
the air like good brandy igniting the brain.

Then we saw it, down on the roadway,
the great blue heron, lord of the marsh,
stalking slow dancer, the totem of this place
shot, lying in his bright light blood.
I laid him on the bank but he was frozen
already. Shot I think at sunset.

I was stropped by rage against the fool
who answered strange beauty by killing it.
I see herons in afternoon pumpkin light
flapping up the Herring River, by the Inn
at Duck Creek, I see them at sunset landing
with a little stiff drop on their marshy isle.

But dawn is when they stand as omens to me,
the biggest near to the dike guarding the flock
that feeds in stippled shallows the tide has bared.
Any day I see you begins blessed, for I pray
by walking, making my nishmat,* and your wide
wings promise me something holy survives.

* morning prayer in Judaism

132

The wind changes

Yesterday the sky was larkspur velour.
The eye sank into it with languid ease.
The sun lay spooned like marmalade on the drifts of leaves.
I found flowers of calendula, orange and green
eyed, the pointy blue of borage, last
brassy nasturtiums, although the first frost
is a month past, the maples plucked.
The broccoli thrust up new shoots.

This morning sleet slithers over the windows.
The wind is spinning around toward the north
like a compass needle quivering.
I see them suddenly on the grapevine—
the snowbirds, the dark eyed juncos,
birds that fly down from the White
Mountains, the Maine firs
bringing the snow south.

They slip in, they join the confetti of finches,
of bluejays and nuthatches and chickadees
around the feeders. Jaunty and meek,
they are the jolly little omens
of hard times coming, warning
to fix the shed door and mulch the carrots
and kale, bring in more wood, for the snow
is coming like an army of occupation.

The pain came back like
something sharp in my eye

I'm not even sure if it's three or four years
since you killed yourself in that town
as familiar to me as my own hand,
on a street I can close my eyes and see,
smell the oaks' crushed salmon leaves
while the air, heavier there, weighs on me.

Suddenly this morning I saw your face
years ago, in Central Park on one of our good
mornings when we could love like brother
and sister. The Mime Troupe was playing.
Everyone was in costume except you, clumping
in your boots. A medieval fair of tattered

squalid joyful finery, feathers, bells,
banners and face paint, an audience
far gaudier than the players strutting,
but you were sternly exiled from the crowd
momentarily happy bound to me, holding
my hand and lolling on the grass

like an off duty Great Dane, paws up and waving.
We worked together in passionate creation.
Our minds embraced in a dance of pythons,
a cool precise joining of armored hides,
swaying and coiling. In high excitement
we built our pamphlets, our articles, theses.

Sex came easily to me as taking your hand.
For you it was a perilous journey

into a wraith land where the self could shred,
rub off, dissolve in acid of emotion.
Only anger felt safe. Once you threw
a stolid office typewriter across a room.

Another time you knocked down a man
who was dancing benignly with me at a party.
You stalked all my lovers with dialectical
cunning. You wanted me to be yours and chaste
as Beatrice in Dante's mind. I seduced
you thinking that would slash through all knots.

You never forgave me paddling in your flesh.
For me it was simple as tossing a shirt over
a chair; for you it was an Amazon jungle entered
at risk of life. You left me covered with bruises
having finally learned that sex is not
a universal lubricant for nervous men.

After that I stood as the wicked stepmother,
the seductive quicklime into which your ego
could slip, and I kept back, guilty because
my naive solution had left me smelling
like rotten onions, your fear a bloody
glue I could not wash out of my hair.

You glowered that everyone was stealing
your ideas. You constantly flung yourself
into new fields. Sociology would provide
the analysis; lay analysis sweated true answers;

answers came from theology or mathematics.
Then you decided only manual labor was honest.

You were an indifferent carpenter, building
ponderous cabinets that could have held
angry elephants or you on a rampage. You
tried plumbing and the water ran down the street.
Bricklaying gave you two broken bones in your foot.
You developed an allergy to water based paint.

You were always immense and sullenly bright,
a sore thumb of colossal proportions.
Your pain hummed like a dynamo at a dam.
There was no way to be with you, for you could
neither love me nor let me be, and the perfect
virgin mother you needed could never be me.

I am angry too, at the waste of you
into a rage that spoiled whatever it loved
like a dog that tears up its own toys and bed.
You feared love with an energy better spent
fearing death, to whom you gave yourself wholly
at last, supine to that sour kiss.

The whale we are

The mind plunges into sleep, lurching down.
The mind grows huge in the night and sings—
too high-pitched, too deep for a waking ear.
Words bob in the shallows but the dreaming mind

dives past drowning. The mind grows a tail
broad and strong enough to smack a wave,
flippers and immense lungs which store air
like a precious oil to use in droplets.

The dreaming mind plummets into water dense
as rock where ancestors forgotten on land
shine dim as fourth magnitude stars sending
messages that the mind suddenly decodes.

We feed there on flesh we would scorn under
lamps, with dishes and tablecloth and salt
shaker ready to give that sea taste to our food.
We battle for mates we would shudder to see.

We lunge upward, we leap and breach and breathe.
The farther we traveled undersea, the fresher
and brighter we waken. We must go down nightly
sliding past the mincing debris of names, clothing,

the furniture of the day and dropping our limbs,
our busy hands, must thrash deep into that sea
we call alien where for hours the mind chases
and bolts somber glimmering ancient prey.

For Mars and her children returning in March

1.

To name is not to possess what cannot
be owned or even known in the small words
and endless excuses of human speech.
I have adopted a humpback whale, Mars.

When I renew my support for whale research
a photo comes, usually her flukes—
diving or perhaps slapping the water.
Fictional bond, sucker bait, gimmick.

Last winter while humpbacks
were washing up week by week, she birthed,
the year of heaviness issuing in life,
her sisters about her attending.

So every spring I wait to see if she
returns, for naming makes valuable to us
what is unique in itself, one of four
hundred and thirty-five local humpbacks we haven't yet killed.

2.

Jonah in the dark
hears the immense heart throbbing like a generator.
Tours the cathedral of the lungs.
This is the Great Kirk of Bavo

baroque organ intricate and massive as a Bach fugue
in the white ship scrubbed down to holy salt.
The air rushes in and percolates,
basalt dense as he plummets past canyons and cliffs.

Jonah sees lights dancing like those lanterns
swinging in the night the mooncussers used to hang
on horses' necks to lure ships to wreck on the great beach.
His nerves explode tracer patterns on his eyeballs.

But now above the sloshing and churning,
the engine of the heart, he hears the voice of the whale.
He is inside the organ; the lungs are its bellows.
Its pipes are fathoms tall.
He is a little cupidon cast from brass as decoration.

He is carried inside a tenor the size of a concert hall
improvising on themes he hears now from all sides,
a chamber orchestra enclosed in no chamber at all.
Clicks, squeaks, moans, trills, resonant as thunder
it sounds electronic.

In the night the tones flicker and shimmer,
fiery arias in the salty dark
nets of sound trailing through the silence
like constellations floating in the wet void.

In the cave of the whale Jonah studies
our elder brother and sister

who went down to the sea without a ship
and swam for the bottom.
Leviathan reaps the wild bounty of the wave,
without nets, without ships, without tools.
Leviathan does not slave or spend
but lashes his mighty tail and sounds
free as we never will be
and loving to his kind.

Our prayers rise like clouds of whining mosquitoes
all day and all night, give me, I want, I need,
I must have him, her, the heart of my enemy,
a diamond as big as Leviathan,
a mountain to strip mine,
whales to harvest, while they sing
a dwindling psalm to the great eye
that watches from inside.

3.

Arcing out of the grey green moil of water
the humpback offers her plume of praise,
steam gusting from the hot stove of her heart.

They are houses leaping,
they are ore boats upending.
Lava flows, they float on the calm.
Leather icebergs, they are sunning in the current.

Breaching, now they travel in bow curves,
viaducts, strong arches of speed,

up and over, rolling into the sea again,
huge smooth wheels turning past us.

Now she rises just beside the boat,
thrusting herself out, dark joy towering
over me where I grip the slippery wet rail.

Her steam touches my face.
Her breath enters my nose and my lungs.
That small vulnerable eye bright as a chip
of obsidian looks at me, sees me
sizes me up, small, pale, staring in awe.

We in our boats permitted among you—
spanking the waves, slamming the doors of the sea—
let us sketch our quadrille on the waves
of Stellwagen Bank where fish swirl and jump.
My shirt is wet with the breath of the whale,
an anointing, a fishy embrace.

4.

Here on this question mark of sand sprawled
gracefully on the tumbling sea,
we know the whales one by one.
In the grim harvest of last winter
the bodies washed up on the bay beaches.

A dead warbler under the leafless bayberry
may provoke us to pass by with the flash

of mourning that flesh shudders out its breath
and turns cold, fading feathers in the brown
grasses dying back. But a dead whale:
a shrieking gyre of hungry seagulls turns
and turns over the heap of it, the eye
still open and not yet picked out.
Soon it stinks like a battlefield.
The bulldozer arrives to labor at burial.

We see the little as cute, the big as impressive
although we are oftener killed by viruses
too tiny for our eye to register without
electronic aid, than by an elephant in must.

But here the loss is not impersonal, one whale
becoming the next, anonymous as rock piles in the desert.
Each is known. Beltane, Comet, Point,
Talon noted among Cape friends dead this cycle.

We must praise each humpback breaching, meet them on the
        banks,
lurch over their feeding on sand lances, herring.
Each is a poet, a composer, a scholar of the roads
below. They are always singing, and what they know
is as alien to us as if they swim past Sirius.

Naming turns the crowd into faces,
turns no man's land into someone's turf,

making a stray and starving cat a pet.
Naming makes a whale who swims through the sea
strewn with human waste and poison,
the trash of boats and cities,
the nets and shipping, known to us,
pod and matrilineal descent, travels
and fate. One community encompasses
this fragile fawn-colored coil of sand
and the vast and roiling Gulf Stream river
and all of us finny, furred and feathered
who dwell in and on this living dying ocean.

If we cannot preserve the greatest of these
from our own greed, our carelessness,
then we will surely follow that shape of natural power
into the silence after its murdered song,
the sea whose hot heart has been stopped
lapping like heavy oil at beaches
where only plastic shards cast up on the stained sand.

INDIGO

The cat's song

Mine, says the cat, putting out his paw of darkness.
My lover, my friend, my slave, my toy, says
the cat making on your chest his gesture of drawing
milk from his mother's forgotten breasts.

Let us walk in the woods, says the cat.
I'll teach you to read the tabloid of scents,
to fade into shadow, wait like a trap, to hunt.
Now I lay this plump warm mouse on your mat.

You feed me, I try to feed you, we are friends,
says the cat, although I am more equal than you.
Can you leap twenty times the height of your body?
Can you run up and down trees? Jump between roofs?

Let us rub our bodies together and talk of touch.
My emotions are pure as salt crystals and as hard.
My lusts glow like my eyes. I sing to you in the mornings
walking round and round your bed and into your face.

Come I will teach you to dance as naturally
as falling asleep and waking and stretching long, long.
I speak greed with my paws and fear with my whiskers.
Envy lashes my tail. Love speaks me entire, a word

of fur. I will teach you to be still as an egg
and to slip like the ghost of wind through the grass.

How the full moon wakes you

The white cat is curled up in the sky
its cloudy tail drawn round its flanks.
Waking, it struts over the roofs singing
down chimneys, its claws clicking

on the roof tiles that loosen and fall.
Now it runs along the bare boughs of the oak.
Now it leaps to the beech and sharpens
its long yellow claws. Sparks fly out.

The moon is hungry and calls to be fed,
cries to come into the bedroom through
the skylight and crawl under the covers,
to curl up at your breast and purr.

The moon caterwauls on the back fence
saying I burn, I am hot as molten silver.
I am the dancer on the roof who wakes you.
Rise to me and I will melt you to silk dust.

I am the passion you have forgotten
in your long sleep, but now your bones glow
through your flesh, your eyes see in the dark.
On owl wings you will hunt through the night.

The hunger moon

The snow is frozen moonlight on the marshes.
How bright it is tonight, the air thin
as a skim of black ice and serrated,
cutting the lungs. My eyes sting.

Spring, I watch the moon for instruction
in planting; summer, I gauge her grasp
on the tides of the sea, the bay, my womb:
now you may gather oysters, now lay

the white, the red, the black beans
into the earth eyes rolled upwards.
But winters, we are in opposition.
I must fight the strong pulls of the body.

The blood croons, curl to sleep, embryo in a seed.
Early to sleep, late to rise from the down cave.
Even at seven, night squats in the pines.
Swim in the womb of dreams and grow new limbs.

Awake at last, the body begins to crave,
not salads, not crisp apples and sweet kiwis,
but haunches of beef and thick fatty stews.
Eat, whispers the crone in the bone, eat.

The hunger moon is grinning like a skull.
The bats are asleep. The little voles

streak starving through tunnels in the snow
and voracious shrews race after them.

Eat, make fat against famine, grow round
while there's something rich to gnaw on,
urges the crone from her peasant wisdom.
She wants every woman her own pumpkin,

she wants me full as tonight's moon
when I long to wane. Why must I fight her,
who taught my mother's mother's mothers
to survive the death marches of winters past?

Shabbat moment

A scarf trailing
over the lilac sunset,
fair weather clouds,
cirrus uncinus
silk chiffon.
Twilight softens the air,
whispering, come,
lie down with me.

Untie the knots of the will.
Loosen
your clenched grip
barren hills of bone.
Here, no edges to hone,
only the palm fallen
open as a rose about
to toss its petals.

What you have made,
what you have spoiled
let go.
Let twilight empty
the crowded rooms
quiet the jostling colors
to hues of swirling water
pearls of fog.

This is the time
for letting time go

like a released balloon
dwindling.
Tilt your neck and let
your face open to the sky
like a pond catching light
drinking the darkness.

Amidah: on our feet
we speak to you

We rise to speak
a web of bodies aligned like notes of music.

1.

Bless what brought us through
the sea and the fire; we are caught
in history like whales in polar ice.
Yet you have taught us to push against the walls,

to reach out and pull each other along,
to strive to find the way through
if there is no way around, to go on.
To utter ourselves with every breath

against the constriction of fear,
to know ourselves as the body born from Abraham
and Sarah, born out of rock and desert.
We reach back through two hundred arches of hips

long dust, carrying their memories inside us
to live again in our life, Isaac and Rebecca,
Rachel, Jacob, Leah. We say words shaped
by ancient use like steps worn into rock.

2.

Bless the quiet of sleep
easing over the ravaged body, who quiets

This was one among many parts written for a Reconstructionist siddur to
be published by P'Nai Or

the troubled waters of the mind to a pool
in which shines the placid broad face of the moon.

Bless the teaching of how to open
in love so all the doors and windows of the body
swing wide on their rusty hinges
and we give ourselves with both hands.

Bless what stirs in us compassion
for the hunger of the chickadee in the storm
starving for seeds we can carry out,
the wounded cat wailing in the alley,

what shows us our face in a stranger,
who teaches us what we clutch shrivels
but what we give goes off in the world
carrying bread to people not yet born.

Bless the gift of memory
that breaks unbidden, released
from a flower or a cup of tea
so the dead move like rain through the room.

Bless what forces us to invent
goodness every morning and what never frees
us from the cost of knowledge, which is
to act on what we know again and again.

3.

All living are one and holy, let us remember
as we eat, as we work, as we walk and drive.

All living are one and holy, we must make ourselves worthy.
We must act out justice and mercy and healing
as the sun rises and as the sun sets,
as the moon rises and the stars wheel above us,
we must repair goodness.
We must praise the power of the one that joins us.
Whether we plunge in or thrust ourselves far out
finally we reach the face of glory too bright
for our eyes and yet we burn and we give light.

We will try to be holy,
we will try to repair the world given to us to hand on.
Precious is this treasure of words and knowledge and deeds
that moves inside us.
Holy is the hand that works for peace and for justice,
holy is the mouth that speaks for goodness
holy is the foot that walks toward mercy.

Let us lift each other on our shoulders and carry each other
        along.
Let holiness move in us.
Let us pay attention to its small voice.
Let us see the light in others and honor that light.
Remember the dead who paid our way here dearly, dearly
and remember the unborn for whom we build our houses.

Praise the light that shines before us, through us, after us,
        Amein.

Feeling quite temporary

The air slices my lungs, dissecting me.
It is steel too sharp to endure.
My eyes are singed with ice and weep.

I walk under the sickle moon sharpened
and new and whistling. The snow creaks
under my soles. Yesterday's footprints

are turned to sculpture, cat's paw,
deer's female impress, raccoon's waddle
and both our tracks in boots climbing.

My words float toward you in clouds
of cooking steam, gauzy puffs
and sentences like wedding veils

slowly vanishing. It is the living
warmth of our hearts we breathe out.
On the white pillow of snow, the fallen

goldfinch lies brilliant and stiff,
hard as ceramic. This season keeps
what it takes like a shell collector.

The warmth of our bodies fades out,
ashy wisps, in the cold that stretches
into the great winter between the stars.

Sexual selection among birds

The soft breasted dun bird on her nest
incubating a clutch of sand colored eggs,
her dreams are scarlet and cobalt.

Her mate is gaudy, enameled like
a Fabergé egg, jeweled and singing:
the artifact of her aesthetic lust.

Over the bower of bush where she waits
he dances in the air, mine, mine:
but she knows better.

Of all the females, she, feathered
dinosaur, is the choosiest, the most
critical, demanding of her mate

not only fidelity, passion, offspring
but that he sing like Mozart
and bloom like a perfect rose.

Imaging

I am my body.
This is not a dress, a coat;
not a house I live in;
not a suit of armor for close fighting;
not a lump of meat in which I nuzzle like a worm.

I issue orders from the command tower;
I look out the twin windows staring,
reading the buzz from ears, hands, nose,
weighing, interpreting, forecasting.
Downstairs faceless crowds labor.

I am those mute crowds rushing.
I must glide down the ladder of bone,
I must slide down the silken ropes
of the nerves burning in their darkness.
I must ease into the warm egg of the limbic brain.

Like learning the chemical language of ants,
we enter and join to the body lying
down as if to a lover. We ourselves,
caves we must explore in the dark,
eyes shut tight and hands unclenched.

Estranged from ourselves to the point
where we scarcely credit the body's mind,

in we go reclaiming what once we knew.
We wrestle the dark angel of our hidden
selves, fighting all night for our lives.

Who is this angel I meet on my back,
radiant as molten steel pouring from the ladle,
dark as the inside of the moon?
Whose is this strength I wrestle?
—the other, my lost holy self.

The price of the body

(The title came from a phrase by Muriel Rukeyser)

1.

The price of the brain is paid in shock,
in drugs that bleach the kidneys;
in the endless echoing loops of catatonia,
a maze without issue where only you pace;
in terror of the shadow that rips
the heart when no beast pads close.

The price of the brain is paid in lies
that slowly dilute the rich blood
to institutional broth; in parlor games
of self-analysis and miniature guilt
playable in any weather with all its holes,
sand traps and obsessive obstacles.

The price of the brain pays out in what
has been conceived and must be carried out
regardless of cost in lives, cancer, poison
in the water, bent genes, stolen future:
the brain's ability to factor in and out,
to see only what it wills to know.

But the price of the body is pain.

2.

The promise of pain lurks in the cell
nucleus, is programmed into the first
flicker of nerve, the first squeeze
of hunger, the very reading of heat
and cold. Knowledge is built of ouch:

160

too hot, too cold, too wet, too dry,
too high, too low, too dark, too light.

3.

Pain is what we can do to each other,
what we can force upon the sentient.
The torturer swells like a balloon
pumped up with blood. As the tortured
wanes, the torturer waxes in false
reflected light. We have devised
vibrators, perfumes, lingerie, satin
sheets, jellies, but the inventions
of pleasure fit into a boutique.

We could erect a Smithsonian of pain's
little helpers, racks, prods, all the
mechanical, electrical, computerized
vehicles for imposing hostile will.
Whole departments of our government
teach foreign police to meter pain.
Governments research hurt, singular
and plural; it is their most reliable
product. Rule is built of pain.

4.

The soft body wants to drink nectar
like a bee and make honey together.
The soft body wants to put sweet fruit
into its mouth and insert in its orifices

things only hard enough to rub pleasantly,
things that smell and taste sweet, salty
or gamy, to push itself into other softness,
to rub and be rubbed, to curl and coil.

But it gets hungry and cannot eat rock.
Only plants turn light into sugar;
we pass the elements among us, and if
a birch did not keen in its way
loudly as a headless chicken,
we could see the entire exchange
as an immense four-dimensional matrix,
a nebula singing like a Bach oratorio.

What can feel, can hurt: in consciousness
begins our dying back to silence.
Pain is the price of the body.
To feel is to feel pain.

5.

So I shudder with superstitious fear,
so I watch the breakers of days roll in
each eating away a little of my life's beach.

Someone who had lived fully, densely
in the forest of the flesh, shall I not
suffer there as greatly and as long?

How can we not fear that it balances
in the crazy court of desire, that for every

joy a mean justice will scrape penance.

Yet it doesn't work the other way:
abused children are not given more love
in recompense; the poor child never

is satiated with toys. Finally we choose
our cancer inadvertently, trading years
for pay, a home for a kidney, a spleen.

The report on my suspect Pap smear
lists women at high risk: those who did
it young and willing, those with many

lovers, those who had too good a time.
And I don't know that I wouldn't choose
it now, head up, eyes forward, hip cocked:

no, I don't want cancer dealt to me
by my local nuclear dome irradiating my ovaries,
from the air, the water, the food

I must take in to live, my body's stuff,
but a risk well chosen, oh that floats
like a bright fuchsia banner over grey printout.

Whether it's AIDS or cancer, let us hope
we sucked the last morsel of pleasure onto our tongue
since we're charged anyhow for living.

Temple, pinball machine, shooting gallery,
vehicle of need and desire, my body, our fate:
that thought is flesh, and flesh thinks.

The task never completed

No task is ever completed,
only abandoned or pressed into use.
Tinkering can be a form of prayer.

Twenty-six botched worlds preceded
Genesis we are told in ancient commentary,
and ha-Shem said not only,

of this particular attempt,
It is good, but muttered,
if only it will hold.

Incomplete, becoming, the world
was given us to fix, to complete
and we've almost worn it out.

My house was hastily built,
on the cheap. Leaks, rotting
sills, the floor a relief map of Idaho.

Whenever I get some money, I stove
up, repair, add on, replace.
This improvisation permits me to squat

here on the land that owns me.
We evolve through mistakes, wrong

genes, imitation gone wild,

Each night sleep unravels me into wool,
then into sheep and wolf. Walls and fire
pass through me. I birth stones.

Every dawn I stumble from the roaring
vat of dreams and make myself up
remembering and forgetting by halves.

Every dawn I choose to take a knife
to the world's flank or a sewing kit,
rough improvisation, but a start.

A Note About the Author

Marge Piercy is the author of twelve collections of poetry, including *The Moon Is Always Female*; her selected poems, *Circles on the Water*; *Stone, Paper, Knife*; *My Mother's Body*; and *Available Light*. In 1990 her poetry won the Golden Rose, the oldest poetry award in the country. Her book of craft essays, *Parti-Colored Blocks for a Quilt*, is part of the Poets on Poetry series of the University of Michigan Press, and she has edited a poetry anthology, *Early Ripening*. She has also written eleven novels, all still in print, including *Woman on the Edge of Time*, *Vida*, *Braided Lives*, *Gone to Soldiers*, and *Summer People*. Knopf published her latest novel, *He, She and It*, in 1991. Her fiction and poetry have been translated into fourteen languages. She is the poetry editor of *Tikkun*. And in 1990 her poetry was combined with Nell Blaine's paintings to create *The Earth Shines Secretly: A Book of Days*.

She is married to the writer Ira Wood and lives in Wellfleet on Cape Cod.

A Note on the Type

The text of this book was set in Century Schoolbook, one of several variations of Century Roman to appear within a decade of its creation. The original face was cut by Linn Boyd Benton (1844–1932) in 1895, in response to a request by Theodore Low DeVinne for an attractive, easy-to-read typeface to fit the narrow columns of his *Century Magazine*.

Century Schoolbook was specifically designed for school textbooks in the primary grades, but its easy legibility quickly earned it popularity in a range of applications. Century is the only American typeface cut before 1910 that is still widely in use today.

Composed by PennSet, Inc.,
Bloomsburg, Pennsylvania
Printed and bound by Fairfield Graphics,
Fairfield, Pennsylvania